Social Studies

myWorld INTERACTIVE

K

SAVVAS

LEARNING COMPANY

Savvas would like to extend a special thank you to all of the teachers who helped guide the development of this program. We gratefully acknowledge your efforts to realize the possibilities of elementary Social Studies teaching and learning. Together, we will prepare students for college, careers, and civic life.

ISBN-13: 978-0-328-97307-1
ISBN-10:   0-328-97307-6
9 20

Program Authors

Dr. Linda B. Bennett
Faculty, Social Studies Education
College of Education
University of Missouri
Columbia, MO

Dr. James B. Kracht
Professor Emeritus
Departments of Geography and
   Teaching, Learning, and Culture
Texas A&M University
College Station, TX

Reviewers and Consultants

Program Consultants

ELL Consultant
Jim Cummins Ph.D.

Professor Emeritus,
Department of
   Curriculum, Teaching,
   and Learning
University of Toronto
Toronto, Canada

Differentiated Instruction
Consultant

Kathy Tuchman Glass
President of Glass
   Educational Consulting
Woodside, CA

Reading Consultant
Elfrieda H. Hiebert Ph.D.

Founder, President and
   CEO, TextProject, Inc.
University of California
   Santa Cruz

Inquiry and C3 Consultant

Dr. Kathy Swan
Professor of Curriculum
   and Instruction
University of Kentucky
Lexington, KY

Academic Reviewers

Paul Apodaca, Ph.D.

Associate Professor,
   American Studies
Chapman University
Orange, CA

Warren J. Blumenfeld, Ed.D.

Former Associate
   Professor, Iowa State
   University, School
   of Education
South Hadley, MA

Dr. Albert M. Camarillo

Professor of History,
   Emeritus
Stanford University
Palo Alto, CA

Dr. Shirley A. James Hanshaw

Professor, Department
   of English
Mississippi State
   University
Mississippi State, MS

Xiaojian Zhao

Professor, Department
   of Asian American
   Studies
University of California,
   Santa Barbara
Santa Barbara, CA

Teacher Reviewers

Mercedes Kirk
Teacher, Grade 1
Folsom Cordova USD
Folsom, CA

Julie Martire
Teacher, Grade 5
Flocktown Elementary School
Long Valley, NJ

Kristin Sullens
Teacher, Grade 4
Chula Vista ESD
San Diego, CA

Kristy H. Spears
K-5 Reading Specialist
Pleasant Knoll Elementary School
Fort Mill, SC

Program Partner

Campaign for the Civic Mission of Schools is a coalition of over 70 national civic learning, education, civic engagement, and business groups committed to improving the quality and quantity of civic learning in American schools.

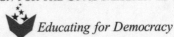

CAMPAIGN FOR THE CIVIC MISSION OF SCHOOLS

Educating for Democracy

🌐 Map Skills Handbook

✏️ Writing Workshop

🔍 Using Primary and Secondary Sources

Chapter 1
Learning and Working Together

GO ONLINE FOR DIGITAL RESOURCES

 eTEXT

 VIDEO

Big Question Video
How do people best cooperate?

 AUDIO

Sing About It! lyrics and music

INTERACTIVITY

- **Big Question Activity**
  How do people best cooperate?
- **Quest Interactivities**
  Quest Kick Off,
  Quest Connections,
  Quest Findings
- **Lesson Interactivities**
  Lesson Introduction,
  Lesson Review
- **Digital Skill Practice**
  Solve a Problem,
  Distinguish Fact
  From Fiction

 GAMES

Vocabulary Practice

ASSESSMENT

Lesson Quizzes and
Chapter Tests

The BIG Question How do people best cooperate?

Chapter 2
National and State Symbols

GO ONLINE FOR DIGITAL RESOURCES

 eTEXT

▶ **VIDEO**

Big Question Video
What does it mean to be American?

◀)) **AUDIO**

Sing About It! lyrics and music

 INTERACTIVITY

- **Big Question Activity**
  What does it mean to be American?
- **Quest Interactivities**
  Quest Kick Off,
  Quest Connections,
  Quest Findings
- **Lesson Interactivities**
  Lesson Introduction,
  Lesson Review
- **Digital Skill Practice**
  Analyze Images,
  Cause and Effect

 GAMES

Vocabulary Practice

 **ASSESSMENT**

Lesson Quizzes and
Chapter Tests

The BIG Question What does it mean to be American?

Chapter 3 Work Now and Long Ago

GO ONLINE FOR
DIGITAL RESOURCES

 eTEXT

 VIDEO

Big Question Video
How have jobs
changed over time?

 AUDIO

Sing About It! lyrics
and music

 INTERACTIVITY

- **Big Question
  Activity**
  How have jobs
  changed over time?
- **Quest Interactivities**
  Quest Kick Off,
  Quest Connections,
  Quest Findings
- **Lesson Interactivities**
  Lesson Introduction,
  Lesson Review
- **Digital Skill Practice**
  Analyze Costs and
  Benefits, Main
  Ideas and Details

 GAMES

Vocabulary Practice

ASSESSMENT

Lesson Quizzes and
Chapter Tests

Chapter 4
Geography of the Neighborhood

GO ONLINE FOR
DIGITAL RESOURCES

 eTEXT

 VIDEO

Big Question Video
What is the world
like?

 AUDIO

Sing About It! lyrics
and music

 INTERACTIVITY

- **Big Question
  Activity**
  What is the world
  like?
- **Quest Interactivities**
  Quest Kick Off,
  Quest Connections,
  Quest Findings
- **Lesson Interactivities**
  Lesson Introduction,
  Lesson Review
- **Digital Skill Practice**
  Ask and Answer
  Questions,
  Summarize

GAMES

Vocabulary Practice

ASSESSMENT

Lesson Quizzes and
Chapter Tests

The BIG Question — What is the world like?

Chapter 5 Time and Chronology

GO ONLINE FOR
DIGITAL RESOURCES

 eTEXT

▶ VIDEO

Big Question Video
How do we track
time?

🔊 AUDIO

Sing About It! lyrics
and music

👆 INTERACTIVITY

- **Big Question
  Activity**
  How do we track
  time?
- **Quest Interactivities**
  Quest Kick Off,
  Quest Connections,
  Quest Findings
- **Lesson Interactivities**
  Lesson Introduction,
  Lesson Review
- **Digital Skill Practice**
  Sequence, Interpret
  Timelines

🎮 GAMES

Vocabulary Practice

☑ ASSESSMENT

Lesson Quizzes and
Chapter Tests

The **BIG** Question **How do we track time?**

Chapter 6

Learning About the Past

GO ONLINE FOR DIGITAL RESOURCES

 eTEXT

 VIDEO

Big Question Video
What was life like in the past?

 AUDIO

Sing About It! lyrics and music

 INTERACTIVITY

- **Big Question Activity**
  What was life like in the past?
- **Quest Interactivities**
  Quest Kick Off, Quest Connections, Quest Findings
- **Lesson Interactivities**
  Lesson Introduction, Lesson Review
- **Digital Skill Practice**
  Compare and Contrast, Compare Points of View

 GAMES

Vocabulary Practice

 ASSESSMENT

Lesson Quizzes and Chapter Tests

The BIG Question What was life like in the past?

Quests

Ask questions, explore sources, and cite evidence to support your view!

Maps

Where did this happen? Find out on these maps in your text.

Maps continued

Graphs and Charts

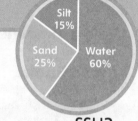

Find these charts, graphs, and tables in your text. They will help you pull it together.

Primary Sources

Read primary sources to hear voices from the time.

People to Know

Read about the people who made history.

Citizenship

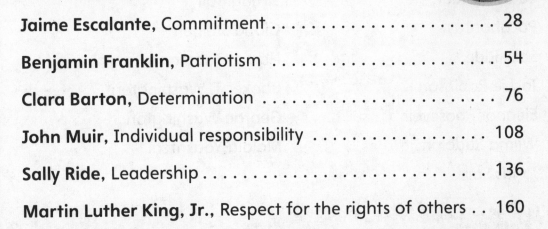

Biographies Online

Bella Abzug

Abigail Adams

Jane Addams

Susan B. Anthony

Clara Barton

Daniel Boone

Chaz Bono

Ruby Bridges

Juan Rodriguez Cabrillo

George Washington Carver

César Chávez

Sophie Cubbison

Marie Sklodowska Curie

Charles Drew

Henri Dunant

Thomas Edison

Albert Einstein

Benjamin Franklin

Betty Friedan

Dolores Huerta

Billie Jean King

Martin Luther King, Jr.

Yuri Kochiyama

Abraham Lincoln

Iqbal Masih

Golda Meir

Harvey Milk

José Montoya

John Muir

Gavin Newsom

People to Know continued

Skills

Practice key skills in these skills lessons.

Literacy Skills

Skills continued

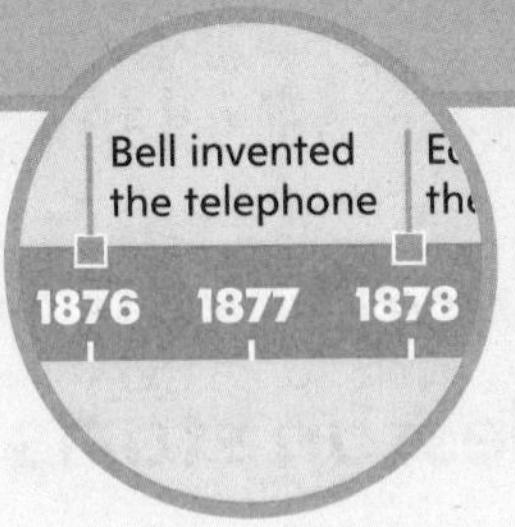
Bell invented the telephone
1876
1877
1878

Critical Thinking Skills

Map and Graph Skills

Welcome to Your Book!

Your worktext is made up of chapters and lessons.
Each lesson starts with pages like this.

Look for these words as you read.

Words with yellow highlight are important social studies words. The sentence with the word will help you understand what the word means.

Lesson 1 Life Long Ago

Unlock The BIG Question

I will know what life was like in the past.

INTERACTIVITY
Participate in a class discussion to preview the content of this lesson.

Vocabulary
history
crop

JumpStart Activity
Act out ways you help out at home.

Life at Home

History is the story of the past.

In the past children helped at home.
They got water from a well.

Today we get water from a sink.
We help wash dishes in a sink, too.

1. ☑ **Reading Check** Underline how children helped long ago.

Food

Families grew crops in the past.

A **crop** is a plant grown for food.
They grew corn and carrots.
They milked cows.
Then they drank the milk.

Today we can go to a store.
We buy carrots, corn, and milk.

2. ☑ **Reading Check** Details Circle crops that families grew.

Reading Checks will help you make sure you understood what you read.

Your Turn!

Flip through your book with a partner.

1. Find the start of another lesson.
   What do you see on the page?

This book will give you a lot of chances to figure things out. Then you can show what you have figured out and give your reasons.

The Quest Kick Off will tell you the goal of the Quest.

You can get started right away.

Watch for Quest Connections all through the chapter.

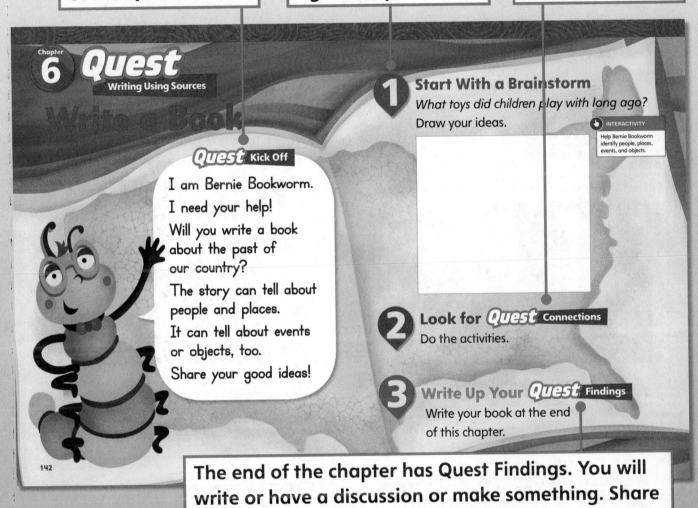

Chapter

6 Quest
Writing Using Sources

Write a Book

Quest Kick Off

I am Bernie Bookworm. I need your help!

Will you write a book about the past of our country?

The story can tell about people and places.

It can tell about events or objects, too.

Share your good ideas!

1 Start With a Brainstorm
What toys did children play with long ago? Draw your ideas.

INTERACTIVITY
Help Bernie Bookworm identify people, places, events, and objects.

2 Look for Quest Connections
Do the activities.

3 Write Up Your Quest Findings
Write your book at the end of this chapter.

142

The end of the chapter has Quest Findings. You will write or have a discussion or make something. Share what you figured out with other people.

2. Find two words with yellow highlight. What are they?

3. Find another Reading Check. What does it ask you to do?

4. Find another Quest. What is it called?

Learn to use important skills.

> Read the explanation. Look at all the text and pictures.

> Practice the skill. You will be ready to use it whenever you need it.

Distinguish Fact From Fiction

A fact is true.

Fiction is not true.

It is made up.

Fact

Fiction

Benjamin Franklin was a patriot. He was a leader of our country.

Jack showed courage. He chopped down the beanstalk so the giant would not get him.

Your Turn!

Look at the pictures.

Read the sentences.

1. **Highlight** the sentence that gives a fact.

2. **Circle** the sentence that is fiction.

INTERACTIVITY

Review and practice what you learned about fact and fiction.

The pigs were determined to keep out the wolf. They built houses made of straw, sticks, and bricks.

George Washington was a patriot. He was the first president of our country.

Your Turn!

Work with a partner.

1. Find another skill lesson. What skill will you learn?

Look at the title. Read about the skill.

Try the skill. Use it when you need it.

Solve a Problem

Dr. Martin Luther King, Jr. was a problem solver.

He was determined to change unfair laws.

He gave speeches and led marches.

He worked with other leaders.

The laws were changed.

You can solve problems, too.

1. Name the problem.
2. Find out about it.
3. Think about ways to solve it.
4. Decide which way works best.
5. Solve the problem.
6. Think about how your idea worked.

Your Turn!

1. **Look** at the picture. **Tell** a partner about the problem.

INTERACTIVITY
Review and practice what you learned about solving problems.

2. **Draw** a picture to show how you would solve this problem. **Talk** with your partner about your picture.

2. Talk about another time you might need that skill.

Map Skills Handbook

Using Maps

Vocabulary

map
legend
scale
distance

A **map** is a drawing of a place that shows where things are.

The **legend** is a list of what the symbols on a map mean.

You can see some cities on the map here.

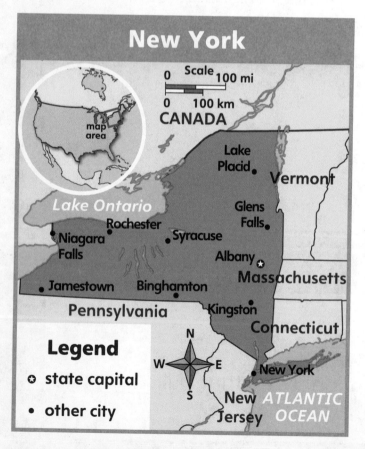

New York

Scale
0   100 mi
0   100 km
CANADA

Lake Placid
Vermont
Lake Ontario
Glens Falls
Rochester
Niagara Falls
Syracuse
Albany
Jamestown   Binghamton
Massachusetts
Pennsylvania
Kingston
Connecticut
N
W   E
S
New York
New Jersey   ATLANTIC OCEAN

Legend
⊕ state capital
• other city

The legend tells you that Albany is the capital of New York.

1. ☑ **Reading Check**
Turn and talk to a partner about the symbols on the map.

Map Skills Handbook

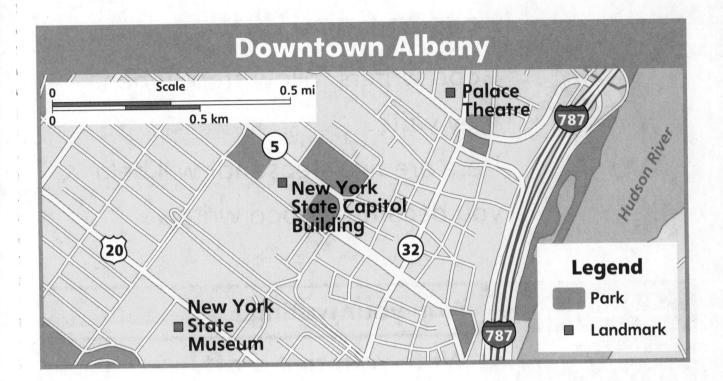

Map Scale

A map includes a scale, too.

A **scale** helps you measure distance on a map.

Distance is how far one place is from another.

2. ☑ **Reading Check** **Find** the scale on the map and **circle** it.

Writing Workshop

Keys to Good Writing

Good writers follow steps when they write.

Here are five steps that will help you become a good writer.

Prewrite	Plan your writing.
Draft	Write your first draft.
Revise	Make your writing better.
Edit	Check your writing.
Share	Share your writing with others.

Kinds of Writing

There are three main kinds of writing.

Opinion

Write about how you think
or feel about something.
Tell why you feel this way.

Informative

Write about a real thing.
Give facts and details.

Narrative

Write about an event.
Tell what happened first, next,
then, and finally.

1. ☑ **Reading Check** **Turn and talk to
a partner about the kind of writing
that is about how you think or feel.**

How Do You Find Information?

You can go to your Library Media Center.

Select a topic to learn.

You can use a computer or books to find information.

Ask a librarian for help.

Search the topic on the Internet.

2. ☑ **Reading Check** **Turn and talk** to a partner. **Name** a topic. How can you find information on the topic?

Be Safe on the Internet

Ask for help if you are unsure.

Never share:

- your full name
- your phone number
- your address
- your birthday

Using Primary and Secondary Sources

Primary and Secondary Sources

We learn about history in different ways.

We can see pictures and objects from the past.

We can talk to our family and friends about the past.

We can learn from primary and secondary sources.

The first hoops were peach baskets with holes.

That is why the game is called "basket" ball.

1. ☑ **Reading Check** **Talk** with a partner about the pictures on this page.

Vocabulary

primary
source
secondary
source

Primary Sources

Primary sources help us learn about the past.

A **primary source** was written or made by someone who was at an event.

A photo and a letter are primary sources.

A photo can show us what things looked like in the past.

We can read a letter to learn about the past.

2. ☑ Reading Check **Turn and talk with a partner about this picture from the past. Ask and answer questions about it.**

Secondary Sources

Secondary sources help us learn about the past, too.

A **secondary source** was written or made after an event happened.

A book about George Washington is a secondary source.

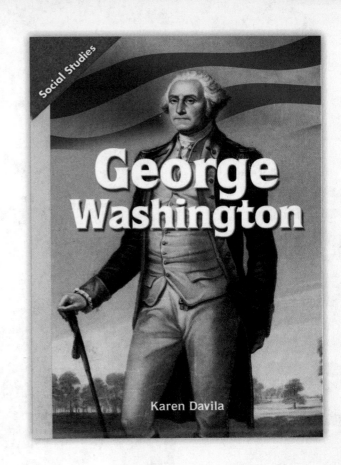

Karen Davila

The writer did not know him.

The writer did not live when George Washington did.

3. ☑Reading Check **Circle** the **picture of the secondary source.**

Learning and Working Together

GO ONLINE FOR DIGITAL RESOURCES

▶ VIDEO

👆 INTERACTIVITY

🔊 AUDIO

🎮 GAMES

☑ ASSESSMENT

📖 eTEXT

The BIG Question

▶ VIDEO

How do people best cooperate?

👆 INTERACTIVITY

JumpStart Activity

Look at the picture. The girls and boys are working together to play a game. Act out how you work together with friends.

 Read along while your teacher reads the text aloud.

We Go to School

Preview the chapter **vocabulary** by singing the song to the tune of "The Farmer in the Dell."

We go to **school** each day.

We **learn** in every way.

We learn to read

And write and spell.

We learn to work and play.

Quest
Shared Discussion

Make a Rule for Your Class!

Quest Kick Off

I am Ollie Owl.
Can you help me make some new class rules?
Rules help us work together and stay safe.

1 Start With a Brainstorm

What are some rules you follow?
Draw your ideas.

👆 **INTERACTIVITY**

Explore the rules you follow at school.

2 Look for *Quest* Connections

Do the activities.

3 Talk About Your *Quest* Findings

Tell the group about your new rule at the end of this chapter.

Unlock
The **BIG**
Question

I will know
how to act
in school.

INTERACTIVITY

Participate in a class
discussion to preview the
content of this lesson.

Vocabulary

school
learn
choice

JumpStart Activity

Turn and talk to a partner. Tell
what you do in school.

What We Do

School is a place where we learn
to read.

We find out something new when
we **learn**.
We learn how to share books.
We learn to sing songs, too.

1. ☑ Reading Check **Talk** about
what you learn in school.

How We Act

We have a **choice** about how we act.

A choice is the act of picking one thing from two or more things.

We can be kind to classmates.

We can help each other.

We can take turns on the slide.

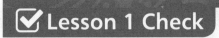
Lesson 1 Check

INTERACTIVITY

Check your understanding of the key ideas of this lesson.

2. Summarize Draw a picture. **Show** a time when you might choose to take turns. **Talk** about your picture.

Unlock The BIG Question

I will know how to get along with others.

Vocabulary

cooperate
problem
solution

JumpStart Activity

Turn to a partner. Show how you get along.

How We Cooperate

It is important to **cooperate**.

We cooperate, or work together, in class.

Then we help each other clean up.

Now we are on time.

We are ready to learn.

1. ☑ Reading Check Tell how the children in the picture cooperate.

How We Share

Sharing is a class rule.

We share many things in class.

We take turns with crayons and blocks.

We share the space around us, too.

Quest Connection

Tell how you get along by sharing with others.

INTERACTIVITY

Learn more about sharing.

2. ☑ **Reading Check Write** and **draw** what you share in school in the chart.

I share	
We share	

What Is a Problem?

Sometimes we have a **problem**.

A problem needs to be solved.

We want to play with the same toy.

Or, we want the same crayon.

How do we work it out?

3. ☑**Reading Check** **Look** at the picture. **Tell** a partner about the problem.

How We Solve Problems

We find a way to solve the problem.

It is called a **solution**.

Think about rules you know.

We can decide together.

We can share.

We can take turns.

 **INTERACTIVITY**

Check your understanding of the key ideas of this lesson.

☑Lesson 2 Check

4. Solve a Problem Act out a problem. **Talk** with a group about ways to solve it.

Solve a Problem

Dr. Martin Luther King, Jr. was a problem solver.

He was determined to change unfair laws.

He gave speeches and led marches.

He worked with other leaders.

The laws were changed.

You can solve problems, too.

1. Name the problem.

2. Find out about it.

3. Think about ways to solve it.

4. Decide which way works best.

5. Solve the problem.

6. Think about how your idea worked.

1. **Look** at the picture. **Tell** a partner about the problem.

INTERACTIVITY

Review and practice what you learned about solving problems.

2. **Draw** a picture to show how you would solve this problem. **Talk** with your partner about your picture.

Unlock The BIG Question

I will know about rules and laws we follow.

👆 **INTERACTIVITY**

Participate in a class discussion to preview the content of this lesson.

Vocabulary

rule
community
law

JumpStart Activity

Act out a way that you and your family stay safe at home. Have a partner guess what you are doing.

Rules at Home

A **rule** is something we must follow.

Rules keep us safe.

People can trip on toys and fall.

We pick up toys so no one gets hurt.

1. ☑ **Reading Check** **Use Evidence From Text Underline** why it is good to pick up your toys.

Rules at School

It is up to each of us to follow rules.

We each raise a hand to talk.

Then everyone has a turn.

Everyone cleans up together.

Then our class stays clean.

We do not run in class.

Then everyone can stay safe.

Quest Connection

What is a safety rule you follow?

INTERACTIVITY

Explore safety rules.

2. ☑ **Reading Check** **Highlight what happens when we follow rules in school.**

School Rules in the Past

Long ago, children also followed rules.

- Fold your hands.
- Sit up straight.
- Stay in your seat.
- Raise your hand to talk.
- Listen carefully.
- Be kind to others.

3. ☑**Reading Check Compare and Contrast Circle** a rule that is the same as a rule that you follow today.

Laws in the Community

A **community** is a place where people live.

A **law** is a community rule we must follow.

We wear a seat belt in a car.

We throw trash in a can.

We wear a helmet when riding a bike.

INTERACTIVITY

Check your understanding of the key ideas of this lesson.

☑ Lesson 3 Check

4. **Main Idea Draw** a picture. **Show** a rule that you follow to make sure no one gets hurt. **Talk** clearly with a partner about your picture.

4 Leaders Make Rules

I will know about leaders who make rules and laws.

👆 **INTERACTIVITY**

Participate in a class discussion to preview the content of this lesson.

Vocabulary

leader
government

JumPstart Activity

Act out a rule you follow at home or in school. Talk with a partner about who made that rule.

Home and School Leaders

Parents, teachers, and coaches are leaders.

A **leader** makes rules and helps us to follow them.

The rules keep us safe and healthy. Rules help us to get along and learn.

1. ☑**Reading Check** **Underline** the names of leaders.

Community Leaders

There are leaders in our communities, too.

They can work in government.

A **government** is a group of people who work together. It makes rules and laws that people follow.

INTERACTIVITY

Check your understanding of the key ideas of this lesson.

☑ **Lesson 4 Check**

2. **Draw** a picture of a leader in your home. **Show** how she or he is making rules or helping you to follow them. **Label** your picture.

Unlock
The BIG
Question

I will know what good citizens do.

INTERACTIVITY

Participate in a class discussion to preview the content of this lesson.

Vocabulary

citizen
right

JumPstart Activity

Act out how you are nice to someone.

What Is a Citizen?

A **citizen** is a person who is a member of a state or country. Good citizens help other people. They follow rules and laws. They work to make things better.

1. ☑ **Reading Check** **Look** at the picture. **Tell** how the people in the picture are good citizens.

César Chávez

César Chávez worked on a farm as a boy.

He saw that farmworkers were not treated fairly.

César felt determined to help.

When he grew up he had courage to help workers get rest breaks.

They got clean drinking water and better pay, too.

2. ☑**Reading Check** **Use Evidence From Text Highlight** how César Chávez helped farmworkers.

Malala Yousafzai

Malala lived in Pakistan.
Some people there did not want girls to go to school.
But Malala was determined to learn.
She gave speeches to let people know this was not fair.

It was patriotic of Malala to help girls in her country go to school.
Today, she helps girls everywhere.

3. ☑ Reading Check **Underline** why **Malala is a good citizen.**

Iqbal Masih

A **right** is what you are free to do.

Iqbal did not have rights as a child.
He had to work many hours a day.
He could not go to school.
Iqbal felt responsible for helping.
Iqbal had courage to give a speech.
He was honest about how children
that had to work were treated.

Now the children have rights.

INTERACTIVITY

Check your understanding
of the key ideas of this
lesson.

☑ **Lesson 5 Check**

4. Solve Problems Tell how the good citizens in
this lesson helped to solve problems.

Unlock The BIG Question

I will read and know stories about good citizens.

INTERACTIVITY

Participate in a class discussion to preview the content of this lesson.

Vocabulary

responsibility

JumpStart Activity

Show how you are a good friend.

The Lion and the Mouse

A lion was asleep in the forest.

A little mouse woke up the lion.

The lion was angry and grabbed him.

The mouse asked to be let go.

The lion laughed but let him go.

One day the lion got caught in a net.

The mouse heard the lion roar.

He cut the net with his tiny teeth.
The lion got free and thanked him.

A good citizen has responsibilities.
A **responsibility** *is something you*
should do.
One responsibility of a good citizen
is helping a friend in need.

Quest Connection

What is a rule that the mouse followed?

👆 INTERACTIVITY

Learn more about being a good citizen.

1. ☑ **Reading Check** **Use Evidence From Text Underline** how the mouse was being responsible.

The Bundle of Sticks

A father had three sons.

The sons did not like to work together.

He gave one son a bundle of sticks.

He asked his son to break the bundle.

The son could not do it.

The other sons could not do it either.

The father gave each son one stick.

He asked them each to break his own stick.

And they could.

The sons were stronger because they worked together.

When citizens work together they make their state or country stronger.

INTERACTIVITY

Check your understanding of the key ideas of this lesson.

✓ **Lesson 6 Check**

2. **Compare and Contrast Draw** a picture.

Show how you are responsible.

Tell a partner about your picture.

Distinguish Fact From Fiction

A fact is true.

Fiction is not true.

It is made up.

Fact

Fiction

Benjamin Franklin was a patriot. He was a leader of our country.

Jack showed courage. He chopped down the beanstalk so the giant would not get him.

Look at the pictures.

Read the sentences.

1. **Highlight** the sentence that gives a fact.

2. **Circle** the sentence that is fiction.

The pigs were determined to keep out the wolf. They built houses made of straw, sticks, and bricks.

George Washington was a patriot. He was the first president of our country.

Quality: Commitment

Jaime Escalante
A Helpful Teacher

Jaime Escalante was a math teacher.

Many of the students in his class had problems at school or home.

Jaime made a commitment, or promise, to them.

He would make sure his class could do hard math problems.

His class had to work hard.

Jaime and his class did not give up.

Talk and Share

Work with a partner.

Tell about a time when you worked hard to learn something.

Tell if you showed a commitment to learning it.

☑ Assessment

GAMES

Play the vocabulary game.

Vocabulary and Key Ideas

1. Draw a picture. **Show** how you **cooperate** with others.

2. Distinguish Fact From Fiction Underline the fact.

The mouse helped the lion get free from the net.

A good citizen is a person who helps others.

3. Draw a line. **Match** a **rule** or **law** to the place where you follow it.

home   community   school

Critical Thinking and Writing

4. Look at the picture. **Tell** a partner how you would solve the **problem**.

Quest Findings

INTERACTIVITY

Use this activity to help you prepare to tell about your rule.

Make Your Rule

It is time to put it all together and tell about your rule!

1 Prepare to Speak

What kind of rule does your class need?

Will you write about working together?

Will you write about keeping safe?

2 Tell and Draw

Use words to tell about your rule.

Draw pictures, too.

3 Share Your Rule!

Read your rule to the class.

Tell about your picture.

Chapter 2

National and State Symbols

GO ONLINE FOR
DIGITAL RESOURCES

- ▶ VIDEO
- 👆 INTERACTIVITY
- 🔊 AUDIO
- 🎮 GAMES
- ☑ ASSESSMENT
- 📖 eTEXT

The BIG Question

What does it mean to be American?

▶ VIDEO

Lesson 1
Our Country
and State

Lesson 2
Symbols of
Our Country

Lesson 3
Symbols of
Our State

Lesson 4
American Heroes

Lesson 5
Our National
Holidays

👆 INTERACTIVITY

JumpStart Activity

These girls are marching in a parade. They are celebrating our country. Turn and talk with a partner. Say words that tell about the country where we live.

 Read along while your teacher reads the text aloud.

32

Holidays Are Special Days

Preview the chapter **vocabulary** by singing the song to the tune of "Yankee Doodle."

Holidays are special days

When families get together.

These are times we share good

Food in any kind of weather!

There are times to have parades

Or have a **celebration**.

There are times to think about

Great people in our nation!

Quest

Project-Based Learning

Guess What?

Quest Kick Off

Hi! I am Ellie Eagle.

Help me look for people and things that tell about our country.

These are symbols.

We will use clues about the symbols to play a game!

Start With a Brainstorm

What symbols are important to Americans?
Draw your ideas.

 **INTERACTIVITY**

Learn more about American symbols.

Look for *Quest* Connections

Do the activities. Find your clues.

Share Your *Quest* Findings

Act out or show your clues to the class. Then they will guess the symbol.

1 Our Country and State

Unlock
The BIG
Question

I will know about America.

JumpStart Activity

Draw a picture of your home. Talk to a partner about it.

Our Country

Our country is the United States of America.

We call it the United States or America.

We live in the country or **nation**.

👆 **INTERACTIVITY**

Participate in a class discussion to preview the content of this lesson.

Vocabulary

nation

1. ☑ **Reading Check** **Underline** two names for our nation.

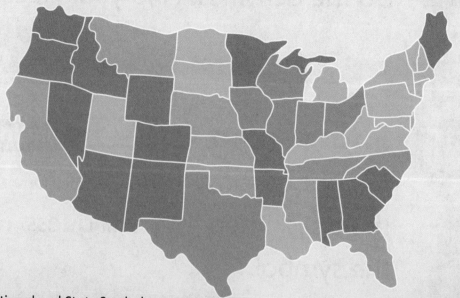

Our State

There are 50 states in our nation.
People from around the world
live in each state.
The United States is their home.

2. ☑**Reading Check** **Highlight
how many states there
are in our nation.**

INTERACTIVITY

Check your understanding
of the key ideas of this
lesson.

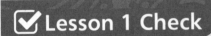

☑**Lesson 1 Check**

3. Compare Think about America.
Write the missing letters. **Talk** about the
people who live in our state and country.

There are 50 _____ tates.

America is a _____ountry.

Unlock The BIG Question

I will know about symbols of America.

👆 **INTERACTIVITY**

Participate in a class discussion to preview the content of this lesson.

Vocabulary

pledge
freedom
landmark

JumpStart Activity

Look at the flag in the picture. Tell your partner about the patterns on the flag.

Our National Flag

All nations have flags.

The flag stands for our country.

We say a **pledge** to the flag.

The pledge shows honor and respect.

Our flag is red, white, and blue.

It has stripes and stars.

It is a symbol of **freedom**, or to act as you want.

1. ☑ **Reading Check** Use Evidence From Text **Highlight** the colors of our flag.

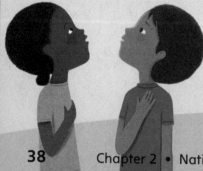

Other Symbols of Our Country

A bald eagle is a symbol of America.

It shows that America is strong and free.

Quest Connection

Circle some things that represent America.

The Statue of Liberty is a symbol of freedom.

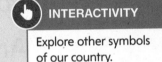 INTERACTIVITY

Explore other symbols of our country.

It is a **landmark**, or an important place.

2. ☑ **Reading Check** Look at the pictures. **Write** the missing letters.

___ald ___agle

___tatue of ___iberty

Songs of Our Country

"The Star-Spangled Banner" is our national song.

It tells about a battle during the War of 1812.

At the end of the battle, the American flag was raised.

America had won the battle.

Many people feel proud to sing "The Star-Spangled Banner". We sing it at sports events.

3. ☑ **Reading Check** **Underline** the event that "The Star-Spangled Banner" tells about.

Other Important Songs

America has other songs, too. "This Land Is Your Land" tells about different places in America. "America the Beautiful" tells how people love their country.

☑ Lesson 2 Check

INTERACTIVITY

Check your understanding of the key ideas of this lesson.

4. Think about the symbols of our nation. Work with a partner. **Ask and answer** a question about one of the symbols.

Analyze Images

Images tell us more about what we read.

We can ask questions about images.

This helps us understand what we read.

What are the people looking at?

They are looking at the flag.

How can you tell this scene took place long ago?

By the way the people are dressed.

INTERACTIVITY

Review and practice what you learned about analyzing images.

1. **Look** at the picture. **Highlight** the answer.

   This picture was taken long ago.
   This picture was taken now.

2. What questions do you have about the picture? **Turn and talk** with a partner about your questions.

3 Symbols of Our State

I will know about state symbols.

INTERACTIVITY

Participate in a class discussion to preview the content of this lesson.

Vocabulary

capital

JumPstart Activity

Act out what you might do with a flag.

Our State Flag

Every state has a flag.

State flags show pictures that are important to the state.

Many state flags use red, white, and blue, just as our nation's flag.

1. ☑ **Reading Check** **Look** at the flags. **Tell** what colors and symbols you see.

Other State Symbols

States have other symbols.

States have a state flower, a state bird, and a state tree.

They have other important symbols, too.

The **capital** is the most important city in a state.

The capitol building is a symbol of the state government.

INTERACTIVITY

Check your understanding of the key ideas of this lesson.

☑ **Lesson 3 Check**

2. Write what you can see on a state flag.

I will know about American heroes.

INTERACTIVITY

Participate in a class discussion to preview the content of this lesson.

Vocabulary

inventor

JumPstart Activity

Think of a person from a long time ago. Tell about him or her.

Heroes of Our Country

George Washington was a brave citizen.

He won a war for our country.

He was our first president.

Abraham Lincoln was known for being honest. People called him Honest Abe. He wanted all people to be free.

1. ☑ **Reading Check** **Underline** two American heroes. **Tell** why they are heroes.

More Heroes

Benjamin Franklin was an inventor.
An **inventor** makes something new.
He helped make our new country.

Pocahontas was an American Indian.
She saved the life of an English settler.
She helped make peace with
the English.

INTERACTIVITY

Check your understanding
of the key ideas of this
lesson.

☑ **Lesson 4 Check**

2. **Choose** a hero from the lesson. **Draw** a
picture of him or her helping our nation.

Unlock
The **BIG**
Question

I will know about national holidays.

INTERACTIVITY

Participate in a class discussion to preview the content of this lesson.

Vocabulary

holiday
celebration

JumPstart Activity

Tell about a day when you get together with your neighbors.

Special Days

Holidays are special days.

We get together with family and friends.

We have parades and celebrations for our heroes.

A **celebration** is a special event.

1. ☑**Reading Check** **Underline** one way we celebrate our heroes.

Washington's Birthday and Lincoln's Birthday

George Washington and Abraham Lincoln were patriotic leaders. We remember their birthdays. We celebrate Presidents' Day in February.

2. ☑️**Reading Check Look** at the picture. The boy is dressed as George Washington. He is in a play. **Turn** to a partner. **Talk** about some other ways you can celebrate heroes of our nation.

Thanksgiving

Quest Connection

Tell about events that are important to Americans.

👆 INTERACTIVITY

Read more to learn about special American holidays.

We give thanks for our food on Thanksgiving.

We remember how the Pilgrims and some American Indians ate dinner together.

3. ☑ **Reading Check** **Highlight the event from long ago that we celebrate on Thanksgiving. Explain to a partner what this holiday means to you.**

Independence Day

We also remember the birth
of our country.
We celebrate Independence
Day with fireworks and parades.
This holiday is a symbol of
our freedom.

INTERACTIVITY

Check your understanding of the key ideas of this lesson.

✓ Lesson 5 Check

4. Draw people celebrating a holiday.
Label the holiday.

Cause and Effect

A **cause** is what makes something happen.

An **effect** is what happens.

The cause happens before the effect.

An event can have more than one cause.

Cause

Effect

Your Turn!

1. Label the picture that shows the cause **C**. Label the picture that shows the effect **E**.

 **INTERACTIVITY**

Review and practice what you learned about cause and effect.

2. Describe the connection between the two events.

**Quality:
Patriotism**

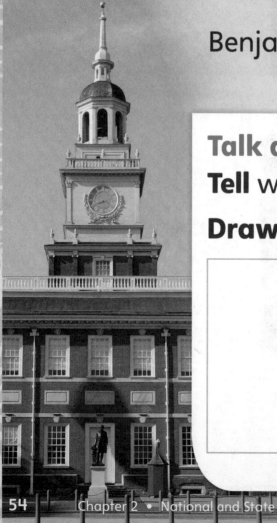

Benjamin Franklin
Patriotic Leader

Benjamin Franklin helped to start our country.

He had many good ideas.

His ideas made our country strong.

He helped write important documents, such as the Declaration of Independence.

Benjamin Franklin loved his country.

Talk and Draw
Tell what you like about your country.
Draw a picture to show it.

☑ **Assessment**

Vocabulary and Key Ideas

1. Draw a line. **Match** each symbol to its name.

Statue of Liberty

flag

bald eagle

2. Circle the missing word. We have **celebrations** on Independence Day to remember American _____.

food

symbols

freedom

3. Look at the pictures. **Write C** for the cause.
Write E for the effect. **Describe** the connection
between the two events.

_____   _____

_____   _____

Critical Thinking and Writing

4. Choose an American hero. **Write** about him or her.

_____

_____ is a hero because

_____

_____

_____

_____.

Quest Findings

Play a Game

It is time to share your clues and play the game Guess What?

1 Prepare Your Clues

Will you draw, act out, or write your clues? Will your clues be about people, things, or holidays?

2 Practice in Your Group

Use words and actions as clues to tell about your symbols. Draw pictures, too.

3 Share Your Clues!

Play the game Guess What? with the class.

Chapter 3

Work Now and Long Ago

GO ONLINE FOR
DIGITAL RESOURCES

 VIDEO

 INTERACTIVITY

 AUDIO

 GAMES

 ASSESSMENT

 eTEXT

The BIG Question

▶ VIDEO

How have jobs changed over time?

Lesson 1
Why People Work

Lesson 2
Jobs at School

Lesson 3
Jobs in Our Community

Lesson 4
Jobs Then and Now

Jumpstart Activity

⬆ INTERACTIVITY

Draw a picture of someone you know doing his or her job.

📖 Read along while your teacher reads the text aloud.

58

Lots of Jobs

Preview the chapter **vocabulary** by singing the song to the tune of "Skip to My Lou."

Baker, **teacher**, doctor, too—

Lots of **jobs** I'd like to do.

Care for animals in the zoo.

What kinds of **work**

Would you do?

What Is My Job?

Quest Kick Off

I am Bella the Builder. My job is to build houses. I work hard every day. What job would you want when you grow up? Dress up and act out the job for friends to guess.

1 Start With a Brainstorm

What is a job that you might like to do?
Draw your idea.

 INTERACTIVITY

Learn more about jobs in a community.

2 Look for *Quest* Connections

Do the activities.

3 Act Out Your *Quest* Findings

Act out your job at the end of this chapter.

Why People Work

**I will know
why people
work.**

INTERACTIVITY

Participate in a class
discussion to preview the
content of this lesson.

Vocabulary

work
job
need
want
cost
benefit

JumpStart Activity

**Act out and take turns talking
about something you can do to
help your family.**

Why People Work

People work for many reasons.

Work is a way to get things done.

People work to take care of family.

People work to make money, too.

1. ☑ **Reading Check** **Main Idea**
   Underline why people work.

Needs and Wants

People go to their jobs every week.

A **job** is another word for work.

A job is a way to make money to buy what we need and want.

A **need** is something we must have to live.

A house, food, and clothes are all needs.

Wants are things we like to have.

A new bike or toy is a want.

INTERACTIVITY

Check your understanding of the key ideas of this lesson.

☑ Lesson 1 Check

2. **Work** with a partner. **Tell** why each thing is a need or a want. **Share** how people can buy them.

Analyze Costs and Benefits

Sometimes you have to choose between two things.

There is a cost and a benefit when you choose between them.

Cost is what you give up when you choose to do something else.

A cost can be money, too.

A **benefit** is something good that comes from making your choice.

In the past, farmers had animals to help them plow their fields. Today, farmers can choose to use machines.

INTERACTIVITY

Review and practice what you learned about analyzing costs and benefits.

Look at the chart. If you were a farmer, what would your choice be: horses or tractors? **Circle** the picture that shows your choice.

Choice	Cost	Benefit
	An animal can get hurt.	An animal can live a long time.
	A machine can break.	A machine can work faster than an animal.

Lesson 2: Jobs at School

Unlock The BIG Question

I will know what jobs people do at school.

👆 **INTERACTIVITY**

Participate in a class discussion to preview the content of this lesson.

Vocabulary

teacher
principal
nurse

JumpStart Activity

Turn to a partner. Tell about the work you do at school.

School Jobs

Many people have jobs in a school.

A **teacher** helps children learn.

A **principal** is the leader of a school.

A **nurse** takes care of the children.

1. ☑ **Reading Check** **Circle** the name of the leader of a school.

NURSE

An Important Job

You have an important job at school.

Your job is to learn to read and write.

It is to learn to work with others.

INTERACTIVITY

Check your understanding of the key ideas of this lesson.

☑ **Lesson 2 Check**

2. **Main Idea and Details Turn** to a partner. **Ask and answer questions** about the schoolchildren.

Unlock The BIG Question

I will know the jobs people do in the community.

Vocabulary

carpenter

market

JumPstart Activity

Act out a visit to a favorite place of work in your community.

Helping People

Many people work in a community. Doctors and dentists keep us well. Police officers and firefighters keep us safe.

1. ☑ **Reading Check Look** at the picture. **Circle** someone that can help if you get sick.

Making and Selling Things

Some workers grow or
make things.
Farmers grow our food.
Carpenters make our houses.

Some workers sell us things.
They work in **markets**.
We can buy food, clothes,
and other things in a market.

Quest Connection

Underline the names of workers who grow or make things.

INTERACTIVITY

Learn more about community workers.

INTERACTIVITY

Check your understanding of the key ideas of this lesson.

☑ Lesson 3 Check

2. Summarize Draw a job in the
community. **Write** the name of the job.

I will know how some jobs have changed over time.

👆 **INTERACTIVITY**

Participate in a class discussion to preview the content of this lesson.

Vocabulary

tool
tablet
smith

JumpStart Activity

Work with a partner. Write and draw a list of classroom jobs. Take turns acting them out.

Work Long Ago

Long ago, many people lived near their jobs.

Teachers and children walked to one-room schoolhouses.

Firefighters went to fires in wagons. Horses pulled the wagons.

1. ☑️ **Reading Check**
Underline the way people got to school long ago.

Work Today

Now people can work far from home.

They can go to school in cars, buses, or trains.

Schools can have many workers in different rooms.

Firefighters go to fires in big trucks.

2. ☑ **Reading Check** **Use Evidence From Text Highlight** the ways people get to school now.

Quest Connection

Tell a friend about a job that uses computers.

 **INTERACTIVITY**

Explore how work tools have changed over time.

Work Tools Today

Some **tools** help people do work faster. Some tools, such as computers, need power to run.

Tablets are small computers. Some workers use them on the job.

3. ☑ **Reading Check** **Details Circle** a tool that needs power to run.

Work Tools Long Ago

In the past, people did not have machines like computers.
They made things with simple tools.

Smiths shaped metal with hammers.
Bakers baked over big, open fires.

Some things took longer to make than they would today.

INTERACTIVITY

Check your understanding of the key ideas of this lesson.

☑ Lesson 4 Check

4. Compare and Contrast Work with a partner. **Look** at the pictures. **Ask and answer questions** about how the job of a teacher has and has not changed.

Main Idea and Details

The main idea tells what a story is about.

The details tell more about the main idea.

Main idea

Detail

Our class went to a busy post office.

We saw computers sort the mail.

Long ago, people sorted mail by hand.

They sorted one letter at a time.

1. **Underline** the main idea. **Tell** one detail.

Our class went to a library.

We used a computer to find books.

Long ago, people used paper cards to find books.

2. **Draw** something that you can find in the library today.

**Quality:
Determination**

Clara Barton
A Very Hard Worker

Clara Barton had many jobs.

She was a school teacher.

She took supplies to soldiers during wars.

She formed the American Red Cross.

These jobs were hard to do.

But she was caring and determined.

She got the job done no matter how hard it was.

The Red Cross now helps people hurt by storms and other disasters.

Tell About It
Turn and **talk** to a partner about how you like to get jobs done.

1134

Disaster Relief

GAMES
Play the vocabulary game.

Vocabulary and Key Ideas

1. You have enough money to go to the movies or to buy a book. **Draw** a picture of your choice. **Tell** about a **benefit** of your choice.

2. Main Idea and Details Circle the main idea. **Underline** the detail.

I have many jobs in school.

It is my job to work with others.

3. Draw a line. Match a job to the correct worker.

builds houses

keeps people well

keeps people safe

Critical Thinking and Writing

4. Look at the pictures. Work with a partner.
Tell how sewing jobs have changed.

Quest Findings

Act Out Your Job

It is time to put it all together and act out your job!

1 Prepare Your Costume

What will you wear to show your job?
What tools will you have?

2 Write

Use words to tell why you chose your job.
Draw pictures, too.

3 Act Out Your Job!

Play the game What Is My Job? for the class to guess.

Chapter 4
Geography of the Neighborhood

GO ONLINE FOR
DIGITAL RESOURCES

▶ VIDEO

👆 INTERACTIVITY

🔊 AUDIO

🎮 GAMES

☑ ASSESSMENT

📖 eTEXT

The BIG Question

What is the world like?

▶ VIDEO

👆 INTERACTIVITY

JumPstart Activity

Take turns with classmates.

Tell about where you live.

What buildings do you see?

Is there water nearby?

Do you see plants?

 Read along while your teacher reads the text aloud.

This Is My Community

Preview the chapter **vocabulary** by singing the song to the tune of "Twinkle, Twinkle, Little Star."

This is where I live and play,
Work and shop most every day.

Here's my home and here's
My **street**.

This is where my **neighbors** meet.

Lots of people live near me.

This is my community.

Quest
Project-Based Learning

Make a Map Game

Quest Kick Off

I am Mateo.

I make maps.

Will you help me make a map of a neighborhood?

It can show homes and a school.

It can show other places, too.

Then we can play a game with the map!

Start With a Brainstorm

1 *What are some things you see in your neighborhood?*
Draw your ideas.

INTERACTIVITY
Identify special places in your neighborhood.

Look for *Quest* Connections

2 Do the activities.

Write Up Your *Quest* Findings

3 Draw your map and play a game at the end of this chapter.

Where We Live

I will know about relative location.

INTERACTIVITY

Participate in a class discussion to preview the content of this lesson.

Vocabulary

relative
location
harbor

JumpStart Activity

Play a game. Take turns telling where something is in your classroom.

Where We Are

Some words tell relative location. **Relative location** is where something is compared to something else.

1. ☑ **Reading Check** **Underline** what relative location is.

Location Words

The words *near, far, left, right, behind,* and *in front of* tell about relative location.

The girl is *near* the fish bowl.

She is *in front of* the boy.

The boy is *far* from the girl.

He is *behind* her.

The fish bowl is to the *right* of the plant.

The flag is to the *left* of the boy.

2. ☑ **Reading Check Circle something to the right of the boy.**

Where Some Families Live

Some families like to live near a **harbor**.
It is a body of water next to a shore.
Harbors keep boats safe from strong
winds and waves.
Boats bring things you can buy.
You can have fun in a harbor.

3. ☑ **Reading Check** **Look** at the
picture. **Circle** something behind
the blue kayak.

Places Can Change

Places can change over time.

A harbor's water might get too low.

People could not fish or boat in it.

Some families would have to move to new places.

4. ☑ **Reading Check** **Use Evidence From Text Highlight** why a family might have to move to a new location.

INTERACTIVITY

Check your understanding of the key ideas of this lesson.

☑ **Lesson 1 Check**

5. Compare and Contrast Draw a picture of your classroom. **Show** your relative location. **Tell** a partner what is good or bad about it. **Tell** how it might change over time.

Globes and Maps

**Unlock
The BIG
Question**

I will know about globes and maps.

INTERACTIVITY

Participate in a class discussion to preview the content of this lesson.

Vocabulary

globe
land
map
neighborhood

JumpStart Activity

Make a list of places you would like to see. Use words and pictures.

Using a Globe

A **globe** is a round model of Earth.
Water can be blue on a globe.
Land can be green or pink on a globe.
Land is the solid part of Earth.

1. ☑ **Reading Check** **Look** at the globe. **Circle** the water. **Draw an X on some land.**

Neighborhood

school

tree

fire station

street

lake

Using a Map

A **map** is a drawing of a place. This map shows a neighborhood.

A **neighborhood** is a place where people live.

This map shows land and water. It shows buildings and objects, too.

Quest Connection

What places would you draw on your map?

 INTERACTIVITY

Explore places on maps.

INTERACTIVITY

Check your understanding of the key ideas of this lesson.

✅ **Lesson 2 Check**

2. **Compare and Contrast Tell** a partner how maps and globes are alike and different.

Unlock The **BIG** Question

I will know the parts of a map.

👆 INTERACTIVITY

Participate in a class discussion to preview the content of this lesson.

Vocabulary

symbol
title
legend

JumpStart Activity

Turn to a partner. Take turns telling what you know about maps.

A Classroom

Look at the picture of a classroom. You can see desks and chairs. There are tables and bookcases, too.

1. ☑ **Reading Check** **Highlight** words that tell what is found in a classroom.

A Classroom Map

This is a map of the classroom in the picture.

It shows symbols.

A **symbol** is a drawing that stands for a real thing.

2. ☑ **Reading Check** **Draw an X on the symbol for the rug. Circle** the symbol for a flag.

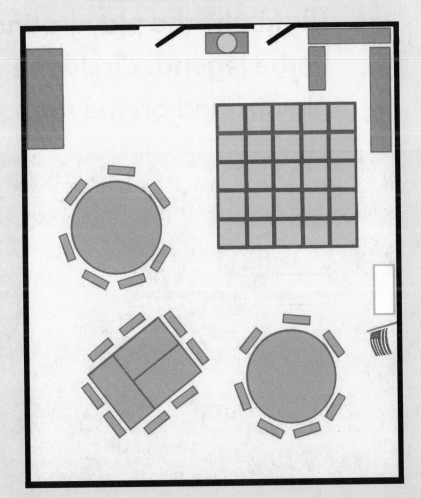

Quest Connection

Tell someone how to get from place to place on this map.

INTERACTIVITY

Find places and things.

A School Campus Map

A **title** is the name of something. A map title tells what a map is about.

This map is titled "School Campus." Some maps have a legend or key. A **legend** tells what the symbols on a map mean.

3. ☑ **Reading Check**

Highlight the playground in the legend. **Circle** the playground on the map.

School Campus

Legend

- school
- bike rack
- playground
- parking lot

School Street

Main Street

Lesson 3 Check

4. Main Idea and Details Look at the map of the nature park. **Make** a legend of things you can find there. **Draw** and **label** your symbols. **Tell** about your legend.

Nature Park

Ask and Answer Questions

We learn more when we ask questions and find answers.

Many questions start with *Who? What? When? Where? Why?*

We can ask and answer questions about maps.

Why is there a star by Atlanta?

We can find the answer by looking at the legend.

A star shows that this city is the state capital.

Georgia

Tennessee

North Carolina

• Dalton

South Carolina

• Athens

Atlanta ✪

• Augusta

Mississippi

Alabama

• Macon

Columbus •

• Savannah

Douglas

Albany •

•

• Brunswick

Valdosta •

ATLANTIC OCEAN

Florida

Scale
0   100 mi
0   100 km

Legend
✪ state capital
• other city

1. Look at the legend to see the symbols for land and water.
Work with a partner.
Ask and **answer** questions about the land and water on this map.

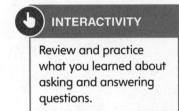

INTERACTIVITY

Review and practice what you learned about asking and answering questions.

2. **Work** with a partner.
Ask and **answer** questions about the mountains on this map.

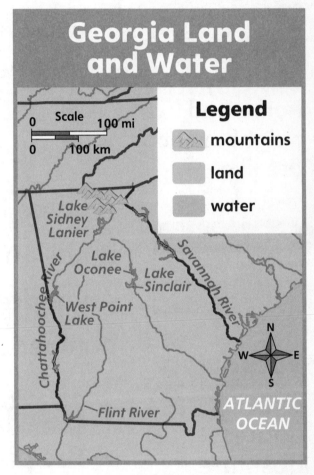

Georgia Land and Water

Scale
0   100 mi
0   100 km

Legend
mountains
land
water

Lake Sidney Lanier

Lake Oconee

Lake Sinclair

Savannah River

Chattahoochee River

West Point Lake

Flint River

N
W   E
S

ATLANTIC OCEAN

Lesson 4
Our Home and Neighborhood

Unlock The BIG Question

I will know what my home and neighborhood are like.

👆 **INTERACTIVITY**

Participate in a class discussion to preview the content of this lesson.

Vocabulary

street
address
absolute
 location
neighbor
transportation

JumpStart Activity

Act out something you can do in your neighborhood.

Our Homes

A home is on a **street** or road.

It has an address.

An **address** tells the street name and number of a place.

1. ☑ **Reading Check Look** at the picture. **Find** and **circle** 8 Elm Street.

Absolute Location

A street address is the absolute location of a place. **Absolute location** is the exact spot where something is found. The Ong family moved from an apartment to a house. Their absolute location changed, too.

2. ☑ **Reading Check** **Work** with a partner. **Look** at the map of the Ong family's move. **Ask and answer questions** about the absolute location of their new home.

8 ELM ST

Quest Connection

Draw symbols for a legend of your neighborhood.

INTERACTIVITY

Explore symbols and legends.

Our Neighborhood

A neighborhood is a busy place!

We can see our **neighbors**.

They are the people living near us.

We can see them shop at

the market.

We can see them save money at

the bank, too.

3. ☑ Reading Check **Look** at the picture. **Circle** places people go in the neighborhood. **Talk** about how people get to those places.

Getting From Place to Place

Our neighbors go from place to place. Some neighbors walk on sidewalks. Other neighbors use **transportation**. A bike is one kind of transportation. So are cars, buses, airplanes, ships, and trains.

☑ Lesson 4 Check

INTERACTIVITY

Check your understanding of the key ideas of this lesson.

4. **Main Idea and Details Work** in a group. **Make** a map of a neighborhood. **Use** the legend below. **Use** your map to make a model with blocks.

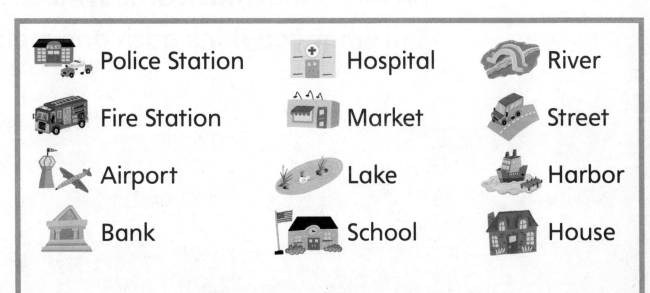

Police Station   Hospital   River

Fire Station   Market   Street

Airport   Lake   Harbor

Bank   School   House

Unlock
The**BIG**
Question

I will know how we make our neighborhoods safe.

INTERACTIVITY

Participate in a class discussion to preview the content of this lesson.

Vocabulary

traffic symbol
ramp

JumpStart Activity

Make a list of safety rules you follow in your classroom.

Street Rules

Traffic symbols are signs.

They show important street rules.

People follow them to keep safe.

A stop sign is a traffic symbol.

1. ☑ **Reading Check** **Look** at the picture. **Circle** the traffic symbols. **Tell** what you think each one means.

Streets for All

Streets are made safe for everybody.
There are curbs and sidewalks.
There are also steps and **ramps**.
Ramps slope down onto the street.
People can roll down them in
their wheelchairs to cross streets.

INTERACTIVITY

Check your understanding
of the key ideas of this
lesson.

✓ Lesson 5 Check

2. Main Idea and Details Draw a
line from the traffic symbol to
the correct street rule.

look for school
children

street goes
one way

stop moving
and wait

3. Talk with a partner about sidewalk ramps.

**I will know
how people
use resources
today and
long ago.**

INTERACTIVITY

Participate in a class
discussion to preview the
content of this lesson.

Vocabulary

resource
lumber
goods

JumpStart Activity

**Talk with a partner. Tell about
things you find in nature.**

Today and Long Ago

Your school has buildings and roads.
But the same place looked different
long ago.
The land might have had trees
and grass.

1. ☑ **Reading Check Talk** with a
partner. **Ask** each other questions
about what the land around your
school looked like long ago.

Resources Long Ago

People changed the land long ago.
They used the resources around them.
Resources are useful things found
in nature.
They chopped down trees for lumber.
Lumber is wood used to build things.
People grew food on the treeless land.
They used river water to cook and drink.

2. ☑ **Reading Check** **Underline** how
people used resources long ago.

Resources Today

We still need resources from Earth.

We use water from rivers.

We use lumber to build our homes.

We grow our food in soil.

But we can go to a store to buy these goods, too.

Goods are things people make or grow.

3. ☑ **Reading Check** Underline a way we can get resources today.

Keeping Resources Safe

We must keep our resources safe.
We will always need clean water
for cooking and drinking.
We will always need healthy air
and land for growing plants
and trees.

INTERACTIVITY

Check your understanding of the key ideas of this lesson.

☑ Lesson 6 Check

4. **Draw Conclusions Look** at the picture. **Circle** the resources you see. **Talk** about how people use resources today and long ago.

Summarize

A summary is a retelling of a story.
It tells the main idea and key details.

In this story, the main idea is underlined.
The details are highlighted.

Daniel Boone, Road Maker
Daniel Boone changed the land.
He made a road long ago.
He did this so more people could move onto the land.

Now read the summary of the story.

Summary Daniel Boone changed the land by making a new road.

Your Turn!

Now **read** a legend, or made up story, about Daniel Boone.
Circle the best summary.

INTERACTIVITY
Review and practice what you learned about summarizing.

Daniel Boone Keeps Moving

Daniel Boone loved the wilderness.
He did not like people.
One day he saw smoke coming from the chimney of a neighbor.
"They live too close to me,"
said Boone.
So he moved his family away!

Summary 1:

Daniel Boone saw chimney smoke.

Summary 2:

Daniel Boone moved as soon as he saw neighbors.

Quality: Individual responsibility

John Muir
Protector of the Environment

John Muir was a writer and an explorer.

He felt responsible to care for land and water in our country.

He helped to form national parks.

He helped to form the Sierra Club, too. It is a group that protects land, water, plants, and animals.

"None of Nature's landscapes are ugly so long as they are wild."
—John Muir, *Our National Parks*

Turn and Talk
Turn to a partner.
Talk about what you do to be a responsible person.

☑ Assessment

Vocabulary and Key Ideas

1. Write the **relative location** of the big sister. Is she standing *behind* or *in front* of her family?

_____

- - - - - - - - - - -

_____

2. Look at the globe. **Color** the **land** green. **Color** the water blue.

North America

Atlantic Ocean

Pacific Ocean

South America

3. Look at the legend. **Circle** the symbol for **street** in red. **Circle** the symbol for water in blue.

Critical Thinking and Writing

4. Work with a partner. **Draw** a map of a parade route in your **neighborhood**. **Use** your map to make a model with blocks. **Ask and answer questions** about your route.

Quest Findings

Make a Map Game

It is time to put it all together.
Make a map and play a game.

👆 **INTERACTIVITY**

Use this activity to help you prepare to make a map game.

1 Prepare to Draw

What are some things you see in a neighborhood?

2 Draw and Write

Draw your map.

Use symbols on your map.

Make a legend for your symbols.

Give your map a title.

3 Play a Game

Share your map with a partner.

Play a game with the maps.

Take turns getting from place to place by asking and answering questions.

Time and Chronology

The **BIG** Question

▶ VIDEO

How do we track time?

👆 INTERACTIVITY

Jumpstart Activity

Take turns with a partner.

Act out outdoor activities you do at different times of the year.

 Read along while your teacher reads the text aloud.

AUDIO

We Measure Time

Preview the chapter **vocabulary** by singing the song to the tune of "Three Blind Mice."

Time can be described with many different words. The **future** and the **past** are two you may have heard. **Calendars** show **months** and days of the **week** that make up the time of **year** you see. There are ten years in a **decade.** That is how we measure time.

Quest
Project-Based Learning

Make a Timeline

Quest Kick Off

Hello, I am Ling Li.
I play outside all year long in China.

Do you like to play outside?

What do you wear if it is cold?

How does it look and feel during the different parts of your year?

Draw me a timeline.

1 Start With a Brainstorm

What outdoor activities do you like to do throughout the year? Draw your ideas.

INTERACTIVITY

Learn more about some activities you can do throughout the year.

2 Look for *Quest* Connections

Do the activities.

3 Write Up Your *Quest* Findings

Draw your timeline at the end of this chapter.

Talking About Time

I will know how to talk about time.

> **INTERACTIVITY**
>
> Participate in a class discussion to preview the content of this lesson.

Vocabulary

present
past
future

JumpStart Activity

Talk about something fun you will do today.

The Present

We use words to talk about time. What happens *now* is in the **present**. The word *today* tells about the present, too.

1. ☑ **Reading Check** Use Evidence From Text **Circle** words that tell about the present.

Present

The Past and the Future

What happened *before* today is in the **past**.

Yesterday tells about the past.

What will happen *after* today is in the **future**.

Tomorrow tells about the future.

Past

Future

2. ☑ **Reading Check**

Underline other words for past and future.

☑ **Lesson 1 Check**

👆 **INTERACTIVITY**

Check your understanding of the key ideas of this lesson.

3. **Compare and Contrast Use** a separate piece of paper. **Draw** three pictures. **Show** yourself doing something in the past, present, and future. **Tell** how the pictures are alike and different.

Sequence

The order things happen is called sequence.

Some sequence clue words are *first*, *next*, *then*, and *finally*.

First   **Next**   **Then**   **Finally**

1. Read the story about astronaut Sally Ride. **Draw** lines. **Match** each sentence to a picture.

INTERACTIVITY

Review and practice what you learned about sequencing.

First, Sally Ride studied.

Next, she went to school to be an astronaut.

Then, she went to space.

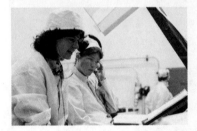

Finally, she gave talks about science.

2. Tell a partner a story about what you have done today. **Use** details and the words *first, next, then,* and *finally*.

2 Measuring Time

I will know how to measure time.

 **INTERACTIVITY**

Participate in a class discussion to preview the content of this lesson.

Vocabulary
calendar
clock

Jumpstart Activity

Act out the things you do to get ready for your day.

Daytime

We can measure time in days.

The sun is up during the day.

It is light outside.

We work and play in the daytime.

1. ☑ **Reading Check** **Circle** the things in the picture that show daytime.

Nighttime

The sun goes down each day.

It becomes dark outside.

We call this time *night*.

We sleep during nighttime.

2. ☑ **Reading Check** **Circle** the things in the picture that show nighttime.

Quest Connection

What are some things you can do at night before bedtime?

INTERACTIVITY

Check out some things to do before bed.

Calendars Measure Time

We use tools to measure time.
A **calendar** is a time tool.
It is a chart.
It shows the days, weeks, and
months in a year.

3. ☑ **Reading Check** **Underline**
what a calendar shows.

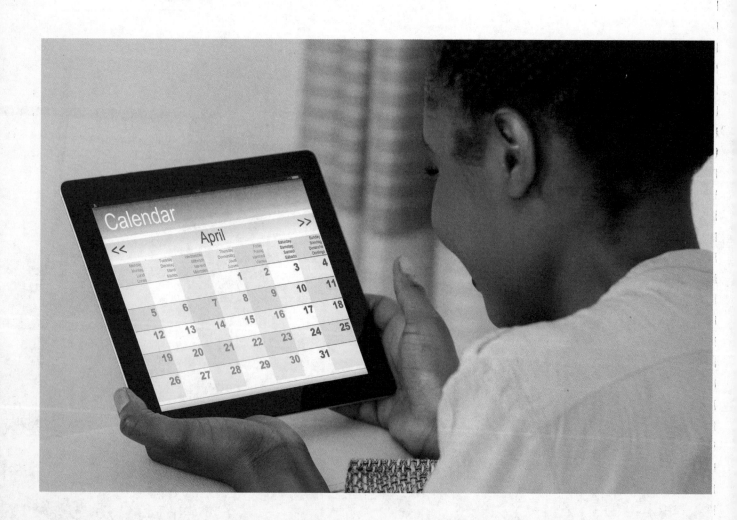

Clocks Measure Time

A **clock** is also a time tool.

It is a machine.

It can tell us the hour.

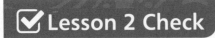

INTERACTIVITY

Check your understanding of the key ideas of this lesson.

4. **Compare and Contrast Draw** the sky during the day. Then, **draw** the sky at night. **Tell** how your pictures are alike and different. **Label** your pictures.

Interpret Timelines

A timeline shows the order in which things happen.

We read a timeline from left to right.

The earliest event is on the left.

The latest event is on the right.

Look at the timeline.

What happens in April?

Put your finger on that month.

Then, look at the picture.

Read the words to find out what happens.

Presidents' Day   Earth Day

January   February   March   April   May   June

Your Turn!

1. Look at the timeline. **Write** the name of the month when we celebrate Independence Day.

INTERACTIVITY

Review and practice what you learned about interpreting timelines.

_____

_____

2. Circle what we celebrate first.

Earth Day   Thanksgiving

3. Draw a timeline of your day at school on a separate sheet of paper. **Use** words and pictures. **Tell** about what you did in school.

Independence Day

Thanksgiving

July   August   September   October   November   December

Lesson 3 Weeks and Months

Unlock The BIG Question

I will know about weeks and months.

👆 **INTERACTIVITY**

Participate in a class discussion to preview the content of this lesson.

Vocabulary

week
month

JumpStart Activity

Tell when your birthday is. Ask if anyone else shares it.

What Is a Week?

A **week** is a length of time.

It is seven days long.

A calendar shows us the days of the week.

1. ☑ **Reading Check** **Look** at the calendar. **Put** an X on the first day of the week.

Sunday	Monday	Tuesday

Days of the Week

The days of the week are in order on a calendar.

The order is Sunday, Monday, Tuesday, Wednesday, Thursday, Friday, and Saturday.

2. ✓ **Reading Check** **Look** at the calendar. **Work** with a partner. **Circle** the day of the baseball game. **Tell** if that day is before or after Friday.

Wednesday	Thursday	Friday	Saturday

What Is a Month?

A **month** is a length of time.
There are 12 months in a year.
A calendar shows the months
of the year in order.
A month can be four weeks long.

Quest Connection

What are
some things
you can do in
September?

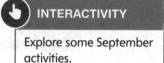

INTERACTIVITY

Explore some September activities.

3. ☑ **Reading Check Look** at
the calendar. **Highlight** the
third week of the month.
Then, **write** the name of the
month on the line.

Month name →

September

Day name

Sunday	Monday	Tuesday	Wednesday	Thursday	Friday	Saturday
1	2	3	4	5	6	7
8	9	10	11	12	13	14
15	16	17	18	19	20	21
22	23	24	25	26	27	28
29	30					

A week ←

A day ←

Day number

Names and Order of the Months

1 January		7 July	
2 February		8 August	
3 March		9 September	
4 April		10 October	
5 May		11 November	
6 June		12 December	

INTERACTIVITY

Check your understanding of the key ideas of this lesson.

☑ Lesson 3 Check

4. Sequence Write the months of the year on strips of paper. **Put** them in order. **Use** a calendar to help you.

5. Work with a partner. **Look** at a calendar. **Find** the month for Labor Day. **Tell** if it comes before or after January.

Unlock The BIG Question

I will know how to talk about long lengths of time.

INTERACTIVITY

Participate in a class discussion to preview the content of this lesson.

Vocabulary

year
decade
generation
century

JumpStart Activity

Work in a group. Make a list of the oldest people you know. Talk about who is the oldest.

What Is a Year?

We can measure time by years.
A **year** is a length of time.
It is 12 months long.

1. ☑ **Reading Check** **Circle** the number of months in a year.

Longer Than a Year

There are ten years in a **decade**.

A **generation** is more than one decade.

It is made up of all the people born and living at about the same time.

A **century** is 100 years.

INTERACTIVITY

Check your understanding of the key ideas of this lesson.

☑ Lesson 4 Check

2. Put the lengths of time in order from smallest to greatest. **Write** 1, 2, 3, or 4 on the line before the correct word.

_____ century _____ decade

_____ year _____ generation

Unlock
The **BIG**
Question

I will know the parts of the year.

👆 **INTERACTIVITY**

Participate in a class discussion to preview the content of this lesson.

Vocabulary
weather
season

JumpStart Activity

Make a list of things you like to do when it rains.

What Is Weather?

Weather is what the air is like outside. Weather changes every day.

Weather is not the same everywhere.

1. ☑ **Reading Check** **Sequence Tell** a partner what the sky looks like *before* and *after* it rains.

Weather Words

We use describing words to talk about the weather.

Days may be *hot* or *cold*.
Days may be *dry* or *wet*.

2. ☑ **Reading Check** **Circle** the wet day. **Put** an X on the hot day.

What Are the Seasons?

A **season** is one part of the year.
There are four seasons in one year.
They are spring, summer, fall,
and winter.

3. ☑ Reading Check **Write** the number
1, 2, 3, or 4 under the name of each
season. **Tell** about each season.

Spring   **Summer**   **Fall**   **Winter**

Weather and the Seasons

The weather changes with
the seasons.

Spring can go from cool to warm.

Summer can be a hot season.

Fall can go from warm to cool.

Winter is usually the coldest season.

Quest Connection

What are
the seasons
like where
you live?

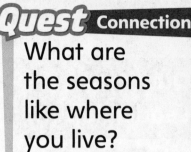

INTERACTIVITY

Help dress for the weather.

INTERACTIVITY

Check your understanding
of the key ideas of
this lesson.

✓ Lesson 5 Check

4. Main Idea and Details Look out
the window. **Draw** what the weather is
today. **Label** your picture with the name of
the season. **Tell** what season comes next.

**Quality:
Leadership**

Sally Ride
A Leader in Science

Sally Ride was a leader in science. She went to school to learn how to be an astronaut.

She worked hard.

Then, she became the first woman from America to fly into space.

Later, Sally started a company. Her company helped girls learn about science and math.

"Our future lies with today's kids and tomorrow's space exploration."
–Sally Ride

Tell About It
Turn to a partner.
Tell about how you are a leader.

☑ Assessment

🎮 **GAMES**

Play the vocabulary game.

Vocabulary and Key Ideas

1. Underline words that tell about time.

present   past   friend

school   century   future

2. Sequence Write *first*, *next*, *then*, and *finally* to show the order of the pictures. **Tell** a story about the pictures.

_____   _____   _____   _____

_____   _____   _____   _____

3. Read the question. **Circle** the answer.

Which is the shortest length of time?

week   year

day   month

Critical Thinking and Writing

4. Look at the calendar. **Underline** the name of the month. **Circle** the day after Teachers' Day. **Draw** an X on the day before May 28th.

May

Sunday	Monday	Tuesday	Wednesday	Thursday	Friday	Saturday
			1	2	3	4
5	6	Teachers' Day 7	8	9	10	11
12	13	14	15	16	17	18
19	20	21	22	23	24	25
26	Memorial Day 27	28	29	30	31	

Quest Findings

Make a Timeline

It is time to put it all together.
Make a timeline of seasons!

1 Get Ready to Draw

What are the seasons like where you live?

What outdoor activities do you like?

What clothing do you wear?

2 Draw and Write

Work in a group. Draw a timeline on chart paper. Draw pictures of the seasons on your timeline. Label your pictures *spring, summer, fall,* and *winter.*

3 Share Your Timeline

Share your timeline with the class.

Chapter 6
Learning About the Past

GO ONLINE FOR
DIGITAL RESOURCES

 VIDEO

 INTERACTIVITY

 AUDIO

 GAMES

 ASSESSMENT

eTEXT

The BIG Question

What was life like in the past?

VIDEO

Lesson 1
Life Long Ago

Lesson 2
People in History

Lesson 3
We Celebrate Our Past

INTERACTIVITY

Jumpstart Activity

Look at the children from long ago.

Act out ways you play with your friends today.

 Read along while your teacher reads the text aloud.

We Share History

Preview the chapter **vocabulary** by singing the song to the tune of "Twinkle, Twinkle, Little Star."

Study all your **history**.

Learn about the past with me.

Study **customs** of each kind.

Study artifacts you find.

Study landmarks everywhere.

History is what we share!

Write a Book

Quest Kick Off

I am Bernie Bookworm.

I need your help!

Will you write a book about the past of our country?

The story can tell about people and places.

It can tell about events or objects, too.

Share your good ideas!

1 Start With a Brainstorm

What toys did children play with long ago?
Draw your ideas.

👆 **INTERACTIVITY**

Help Bernie Bookworm identify people, places, events, and objects.

2 Look for *Quest* Connections

Do the activities.

3 Write Up Your *Quest* Findings

Write your book at the end of this chapter.

Lesson 1 | Life Long Ago

Unlock The BIG Question

I will know what life was like in the past.

 **INTERACTIVITY**

Participate in a class discussion to preview the content of this lesson.

Vocabulary

history
crop

JumpStart Activity

Act out ways you help out at home.

Life at Home

History is the story of the past.

In the past children helped at home.
They got water from a well.

Today we get water from a sink.
We help wash dishes in a sink, too.

1. ☑ **Reading Check** **Underline** how children helped long ago.

Food

Families grew crops in the past.

A **crop** is a plant grown for food.

They grew corn and carrots.

They milked cows.

Then they drank the milk.

Today we can go to a store.

We buy carrots, corn, and milk.

2. ☑ **Reading Check** **Details** **Circle** crops that families grew.

Clothing

Families made their own clothing in the past.

They used their hands to sew.

Today most families buy clothing.

Some families use machines to make clothing.

3. ☑ **Reading Check** **Look** at the picture. **Circle** what people used to make clothing.

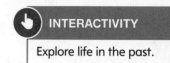
Quest Connection

Circle a toy that children played with long ago.

INTERACTIVITY

Explore life in the past.

Having Fun

Children played games.

They played rolling the hoop.

Today some children play games on computers.

INTERACTIVITY

Check your understanding of the key ideas of this lesson.

☑ **Lesson 1 Check**

4. Compare and Contrast Draw something you do for fun that is different from the past. **Tell** a partner about your drawing.

Compare and Contrast

Some things are similar, or like each other.

Some things are different, or not like each other.

Both pictures show homes.

How are they similar and different?

Long Ago 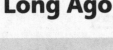   **Today**

This home is made of logs.
One family lived here.

This home is made of bricks.
Many families live here.

1. What do both pictures show?

Work with a partner.

Tell how they are similar and different.

Tell how they have changed over time.

👆 **INTERACTIVITY**

Review and practice what you learned about comparing and contrasting.

2. Write about something from each picture that has stayed the same over time.

_____

- - - - - - - - - - - - - - - - - - -

_____

2 People in History

Unlock The BIG Question

I will know about people who helped our country in the past.

INTERACTIVITY

Participate in a class discussion to preview the content of this lesson.

Vocabulary

explorer
volunteer

JumpStart Activity

Show what you do when you go to a new place.

Daniel Boone

An **explorer** goes to new places.

Daniel Boone was an explorer.

He went on many adventures.

He helped build roads in new places.

He helped others make new homes.

1. ☑ **Reading Check** Underline how Daniel Boone helped others.

Clara Barton

A **volunteer** works for free to
help others.

Clara Barton was a volunteer.

She helped soldiers during a war.

She gave them food and clothing.

Clara cooked and read to them.

She wrote letters to their families.

2. ☑ **Reading Check Summarize**
Draw a picture. **Show** how Clara
Barton helped others. **Tell** a
partner about your drawing.

Quest Connection

Underline two ways Booker T. Washington spent his time as a boy.

INTERACTIVITY

Show your understanding of the life of Booker T. Washington.

Booker T. Washington

Booker T. Washington helped many people to learn.

He wanted to go to school as a boy, but his family was very poor.
He had to go to work.
His mother knew he wanted to learn.
She got him a book.
Booker learned how to read.

3. ☑ **Reading Check** **Circle** why Booker's mother got him a book.

A New School

Booker became a teacher. Then he became the leader of a new school. It was for African Americans.

Booker became an important leader of the African American community.

INTERACTIVITY

Check your understanding of the key ideas of this lesson.

☑ Lesson 2 Check

4. Compare and Contrast
Write how Clara Barton and Booker T. Washington were similar.

_____

_____

_____

_____

5. Finish this sentence. An explorer is someone

who goes to _____

Unlock
The BIG Question

I will know how we celebrate our past.

INTERACTIVITY

Participate in a class discussion to preview the content of this lesson.

Vocabulary

custom
veteran

······················
JumPstart Activity

Show how you celebrate a holiday.

Columbus Day

Christopher Columbus was an explorer from long ago.

He sailed across the ocean.

He looked for new places.

He came to the Americas.

Columbus Day is in October.

1. ☑ **Reading Check Circle** what Christopher Columbus did.

Labor Day

Many people work in our country.

They make our country run.

It is a custom to rest on Labor Day.

A **custom** is the way people

usually do something.

Some workers spend time with

family on this day.

Labor Day is in September.

2. ☑ **Reading Check** **Summarize**
Turn to a partner. **Talk** about
why we honor workers on
Labor Day.

Days for Our Soldiers

We honor soldiers on Memorial Day and Veterans Day.

A **veteran** was once a soldier. Soldiers fight in our wars. They help keep us safe. Many people have parades on these holidays.

Memorial Day is in May. Veterans Day is in November.

3. ☑**Reading Check** **Draw** a picture. **Show** how we honor our veterans. **Tell** a partner about your picture.

Dr. Martin Luther King, Jr. Day

Dr. King helped our country
change unfair rules and laws.
He believed in respect and
fairness for all people.
He worked for equal rights.

We celebrate Dr. King in January.

INTERACTIVITY

Check your understanding of the key ideas of this lesson.

✔ **Lesson 3 Check**
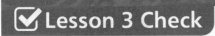

**4. Compare and Contrast
Complete the sentence.** Veterans Day and
Memorial Day both honor

Compare Points of View

A **point of view** is how a person thinks or feels about something.

Some people may agree with you. Other people may not.

Alma and Dion's class is putting on a play about American celebrations.

They have different points of view about how to start the show.

I feel we should sing a song.

Dion

I think we should wave the flag.

Alma

Your Turn!

1. How would you start the play about American celebrations? **Draw** a picture.

INTERACTIVITY

Review and practice what you learned about point of view.

2. Does your point of view match Alma's or Dion's? Or is it different? **Write** your point of view. **Turn** and **talk** to a partner about it.

I think ______________________________

______________________________.

Dr. Martin Luther King, Jr.
Hero to Many People

Quality:
Respect for the rights of others

Dr. Martin Luther King, Jr. was a hero. He wanted all people to be treated with respect.

He and other leaders worked hard to change unfair rules and laws.

They wanted all people to be treated the same.

Today African Americans have made great steps toward equal rights.

Talk and Draw
Tell how you respect others.
Draw a picture to show it.

☑ Assessment

⊕ **GAME**

Play the vocabulary game.

Vocabulary and Key Ideas

1. Draw a picture of a **holiday** you celebrate. **Tell** a partner why it is important.

2. Compare and Contrast Circle one way both items are similar.

Both are old.

Both are phones.

3. Draw a line.

Match the person to what she or he did in the past.

 Booker T. Washington   helped sick soldiers.

 Daniel Boone   led a school.

 Clara Barton   built new roads and homes.

Critical Thinking and Writing

4. Look at the picture. **Talk** about how life was the same and different long ago from today.

Quest Findings

Write Your Book

It is time to put it all together and write your book!

1 Prepare to Write

Will you write about people or places from long ago? Will you write about objects or events?

2 Write

Use words to tell about the past.
Draw pictures, too.

3 Share Your Book!

Read your book to a parent or another class.
Tell about each picture.

The United States of America, Political

DA

Minnesota

Wisconsin

Michigan

Iowa

Illinois

Indiana Ohio

Missouri

Kentucky

ma

Arkansas

Tennessee

Mississippi

Alabama

Louisiana

Georgia

Florida

New Hampshire

Vermont

Maine

New York

Massachusetts

Pennsylvania

Rhode Island

Connecticut

New Jersey

Delaware

West
Virginia

Maryland

Washington, D.C.

Virginia

North
Carolina

South
Carolina

ATLANTIC
OCEAN

Gulf of
Mexico

N

W   E

S

Legend

⭐ National
capital

Gulf of
Mexico

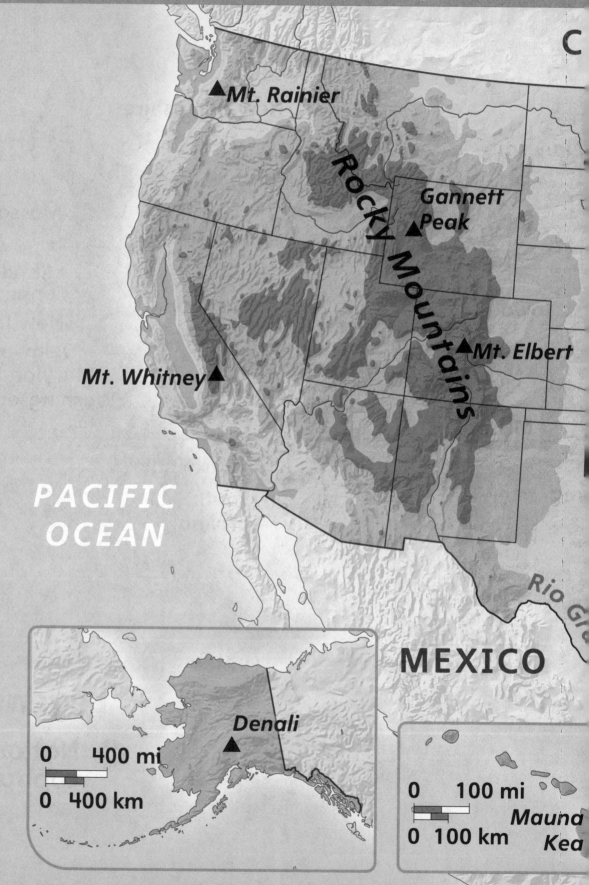

▲ Mt. Rainier

C

Gannett
Peak ▲

▲ Mt. Elbert

Rocky Mountains

Mt. Whitney ▲

PACIFIC
OCEAN

Rio Gra

MEXICO

Denali ▲

0   400 mi

0   400 km

0   100 mi

Mauna
Kea

0   100 km

R2

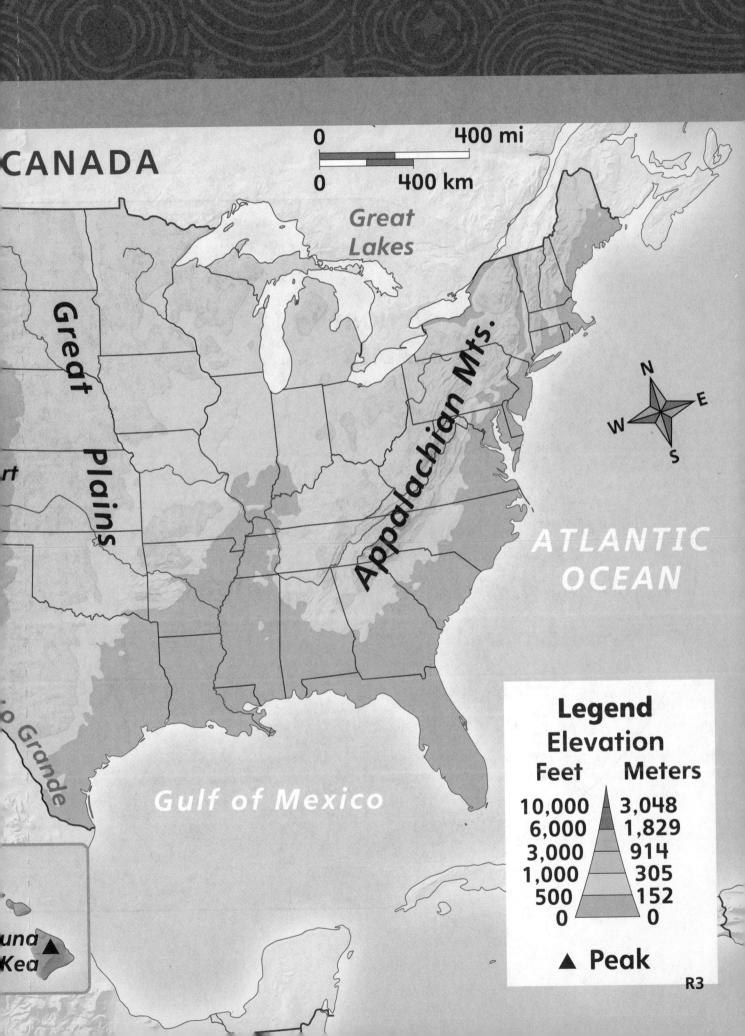

CANADA

Great
Lakes

Great

Plains

Appalachian Mts.

ATLANTIC
OCEAN

N
E
W
S

Rio Grande

rt

Gulf of Mexico

una
Kea

Legend
Elevation

Feet	Meters
10,000	3,048
6,000	1,829
3,000	914
1,000	305
500	152
0	0

▲ Peak

0 —————— 400 mi

0 —————— 400 km

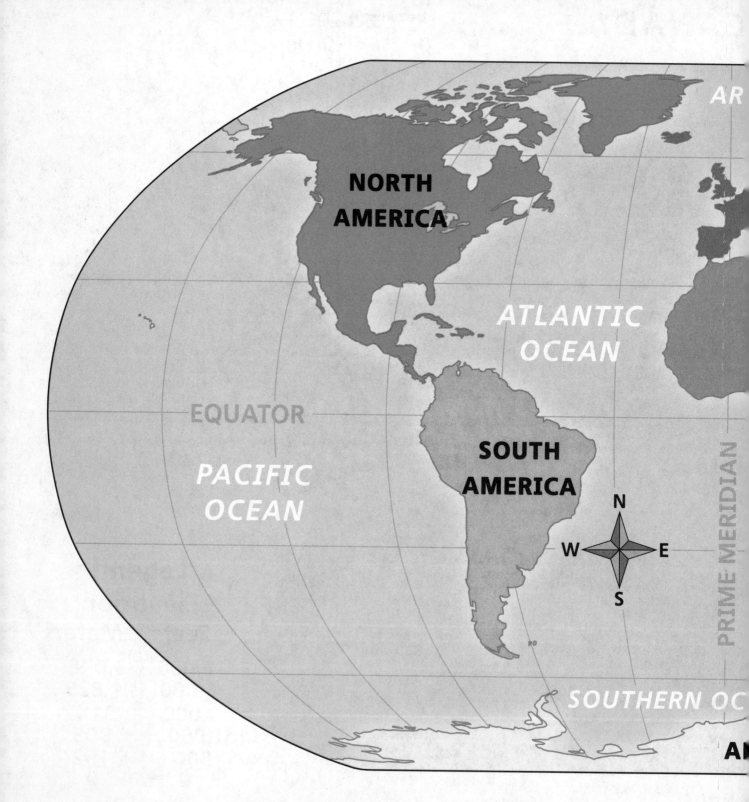

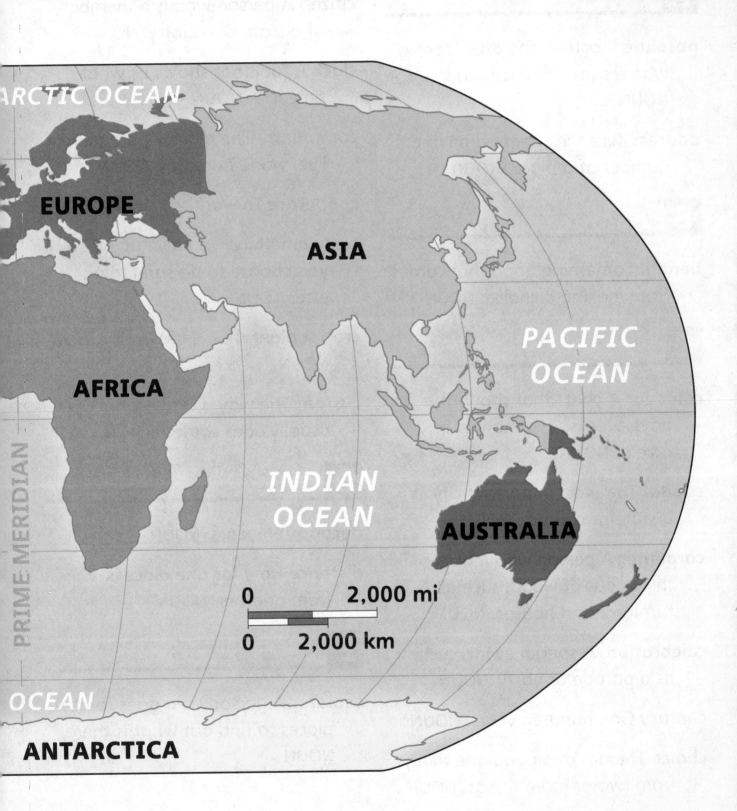

ARCTIC OCEAN

EUROPE

ASIA

PACIFIC
OCEAN

AFRICA

INDIAN
OCEAN

AUSTRALIA

PRIME MERIDIAN

0   2,000 mi

0   2,000 km

OCEAN

ANTARCTICA

Glossary

A

absolute location The exact spot where something is found. NOUN

address Tells the street name and number of a place. NOUN

B

benefit Something good that comes from making a choice. NOUN

C

calendar A chart that shows the days, weeks, and months in a year. NOUN

capital The most important city in a state or country. NOUN

carpenter A person who makes things out of wood, such as furniture and houses. NOUN

celebration A special event, such as a parade or party. NOUN

century One hundred years. NOUN

choice The act of picking one thing from two or more things. NOUN

citizen A person who is a member of a state or country. NOUN

clock A tool that shows us what time it is. NOUN

community The place where people live, work, and play. NOUN

cooperate To work together. VERB

cost Something you give up when you choose to do something else. NOUN

crop A plant that is grown for food. NOUN

custom The way a group of people usually does something. NOUN

D

decade Ten years. NOUN

distance How far one place is from another. NOUN

E

explorer A person who goes to new places to find out what is there. NOUN

F

freedom The right to act, speak, or think as we want. NOUN

future What will happen after today. NOUN

G

generation People born and living at about the same time. NOUN

globe A round model of Earth; it shows land and water on Earth. NOUN

goods Something that workers make or grow. NOUN

government A group of people who work together to make rules and laws. NOUN

H

harbor A body of water next to a shore that keeps boats safe from strong winds and waves. NOUN

history The story of people, places, and events from the past. NOUN

holiday A special day to remember someone or something. NOUN

I

inventor A person who makes something new. NOUN

J

job A way to get things done; another word for work. NOUN

L

land The solid part of Earth where people live. NOUN

landmark An important place. NOUN

law A rule that everyone in a community must follow. NOUN

leader A person who makes rules and helps people to follow them. NOUN

learn To find out something. VERB

legend A list of what symbols on a map mean. NOUN

lumber Wood used to build things. NOUN

M

map A drawing of a place that shows where things are. NOUN

market A place where you can buy things such as food and clothes. NOUN

month A length of time that is about four weeks. NOUN

N

nation Another word for country. NOUN

need Something a person must have to live. NOUN

neighbor A person who lives near someone else. NOUN

neighborhood A place where people live. NOUN

nurse A person who takes care of sick or hurt children in school. NOUN

P

past What has happened before today. NOUN

pledge A promise to be loyal and respectful. NOUN

present The time that is happening now. NOUN

primary source Something written or made by someone who was at an event. NOUN

principal The main leader of a school. NOUN

problem Something that needs to be solved. NOUN

R

ramp A sloped walkway for people in wheelchairs. NOUN

relative location Where something is compared to something else. NOUN

resource Something useful found in nature. NOUN

responsibility Something a person should do. NOUN

right Something a person is free to do or have. NOUN

rule Something we must follow. NOUN

S

scale A way to measure distance on a map. NOUN

school A place where people learn to read. NOUN

season One part of the year: spring, summer, fall, and winter. NOUN

secondary source Something written or made by someone after an event happened. NOUN

smith A person who shapes metal with simple tools such as a hammer. NOUN

solution A way to solve a problem. NOUN

street A road. NOUN

symbol A drawing that stands for a real thing. NOUN

tablet A kind of small computer. NOUN

teacher A person who helps children to learn. NOUN

title The name of something, such as a book or map, that tells what it is about. NOUN

tool Something that helps people to work faster, such as a computer. NOUN

traffic symbol A sign that shows a street safety rule. NOUN

transportation A way to get from place to place. NOUN

veteran A person who was once a soldier. NOUN

volunteer A person who works for free to help others. NOUN

want Something a person would like to have. NOUN

weather What the air is like outside at a certain place and time. NOUN

week A length of time that is seven days long. NOUN

work A way to get things done. NOUN

Y

year A length of time that is 12 months long. NOUN

Glosario

A

absolute location/ubicación absoluta El punto exacto donde se encuentra algo. SUSTANTIVO

address/dirección Indica la calle y el número de un lugar. SUSTANTIVO

B

benefit/beneficio Algo bueno que ocurre como consecuencia de una decisión. SUSTANTIVO

C

calendar/calendario Un cuadro que muestra los días, las semanas y los meses de un año. SUSTANTIVO

capital/capital La ciudad más importante de un estado o un país. SUSTANTIVO

carpenter/carpintero Una persona que construye cosas con madera, como muebles y casas. SUSTANTIVO

celebration/celebración Un evento especial, como un desfile o una fiesta. SUSTANTIVO

century/siglo Cien años. SUSTANTIVO

choice/elección La acción de elegir una cosa de entre dos o más cosas. SUSTANTIVO

citizen/ciudadano Persona que es miembro de un estado o un país. SUSTANTIVO

clock/reloj Instrumento que dice la hora. SUSTANTIVO

community/comunidad Lugar donde las personas viven, trabajan y juegan. SUSTANTIVO

cooperate/cooperar Trabajar juntos. VERBO

cost/costo Algo que tienes que dejar cuando eliges hacer algo. SUSTANTIVO

crop/cultivo Planta que se produce como alimento. SUSTANTIVO

custom/costumbre La manera en la que un grupo de personas suele hacer algo. SUSTANTIVO

D

decade/década Diez años. SUSTANTIVO

distance/distancia Qué tan lejos está un lugar de otro. SUSTANTIVO

E

explorer/explorador Persona que va a lugares nuevos para ver qué hay allí. SUSTANTIVO

F

freedom/libertad El derecho de actuar, hablar o pensar como uno quiere. SUSTANTIVO

future/futuro Lo que ocurrirá después de hoy. SUSTANTIVO

G

generation/generación Personas que nacieron y viven aproximadamente en la misma época. SUSTANTIVO

globe/globo terráqueo Un modelo de la Tierra en forma de esfera; muestra el suelo y el agua en la Tierra. SUSTANTIVO

goods/bienes Algo que producen los trabajadores. SUSTANTIVO

government/gobierno Grupo de personas que trabaja en conjunto para crear reglas y leyes. SUSTANTIVO

H

harbor/bahía Masa de agua que está junto a una costa y que protege a los barcos de vientos fuertes y olas. SUSTANTIVO

history/historia El relato de lo que ocurrió con las personas, los lugares y los sucesos del pasado. SUSTANTIVO

holiday/día festivo Un día especial para recordar a alguien o algo. SUSTANTIVO

I

inventor/inventor Persona que crea algo nuevo. SUSTANTIVO

J

job/empleo Una manera de hacer las cosas; otra palabra para trabajo. SUSTANTIVO

L

land/suelo La parte sólida de la Tierra, donde viven las personas. SUSTANTIVO

landmark/sitio de interés Un lugar importante. SUSTANTIVO

law/ley Una regla que todos en una comunidad deben seguir. SUSTANTIVO

leader/líder Persona que crea reglas y ayuda a las personas a seguirlas. SUSTANTIVO

learn/aprender Enterarse de algo. VERBO

legend/leyenda Una lista de lo que significan los símbolos de un mapa. SUSTANTIVO

lumber/tablas Madera que se usa para construir cosas. SUSTANTIVO

M

map/mapa Dibujo de un lugar que muestra dónde están las cosas. SUSTANTIVO

market/mercado Lugar donde se pueden comprar cosas como comida y ropa. SUSTANTIVO

month/mes Medida de tiempo que corresponde a unas cuatro semanas. SUSTANTIVO

N

nation/nación Otra palabra para país. SUSTANTIVO

need/necesidad Algo que una persona debe tener para vivir. SUSTANTIVO

neighbor/vecino Una persona que vive cerca de otra persona. SUSTANTIVO

neighborhood/vecindario Lugar donde viven familias. SUSTANTIVO

nurse/enfermera Persona que se ocupa de cuidar a los niños enfermos o lastimados en la escuela. SUSTANTIVO

P

past/pasado Lo que ocurrió antes de hoy. SUSTANTIVO

pledge/juramento Promesa de ser fiel a algo y respetarlo. SUSTANTIVO

present/presente La época que ocurre ahora. SUSTANTIVO

primary source/fuente primaria Algo escrito o hecho por alguien que estuvo en un suceso. SUSTANTIVO

principal/director La autoridad principal de una escuela. SUSTANTIVO

problem/problema Algo que hay que resolver. SUSTANTIVO

R

ramp/rampa Un acceso con pendiente para personas en silla de ruedas. SUSTANTIVO

relative location/ubicación relativa Dónde está algo en comparación con otra cosa. SUSTANTIVO

resource/recurso Algo útil que se encuentra en la naturaleza. SUSTANTIVO

responsibility/responsabilidad Algo que una persona debe hacer. SUSTANTIVO

right/derecho Algo que una persona es libre de hacer o tener. SUSTANTIVO

rule/regla Algo que debemos cumplir. SUSTANTIVO

S

scale/escala Una manera de medir distancias en un mapa. SUSTANTIVO

school/escuela Un lugar donde las personas aprenden a leer. SUSTANTIVO

season/estación Una parte del año: primavera, verano, otoño e invierno. SUSTANTIVO

secondary source/fuente secundaria Algo escrito o hecho por alguien después de que ocurrió un suceso. SUSTANTIVO

smith/herrero Persona que da forma al metal con herramientas simples tales como un martillo. SUSTANTIVO

solution/solución Una manera de resolver un problema. SUSTANTIVO

street/calle Un camino. SUSTANTIVO

symbol/símbolo Dibujo que representa algo real. SUSTANTIVO

tablet/tableta Un tipo de computadora pequeña. SUSTANTIVO

teacher/maestro Persona que ayuda a los niños a aprender. SUSTANTIVO

title/título El nombre de algo, como un libro o un mapa, que indica de qué se trata. SUSTANTIVO

tool/herramienta Algo que ayuda a las personas a trabajar más rápido, como por ejemplo una computadora. SUSTANTIVO

traffic symbol/señal de tráfico Una señal que muestra una regla de seguridad en la calle. SUSTANTIVO

transportation/medio de transporte Una manera de llegar de un lugar a otro. SUSTANTIVO

veteran/veterano Persona que fue un soldado en el pasado. SUSTANTIVO

volunteer/voluntario Persona que trabaja para ayudar a otros sin recibir dinero a cambio. SUSTANTIVO

want/deseo Algo que a una persona le gustaría tener. SUSTANTIVO

weather/estado del tiempo Cómo está el aire afuera en un lugar a cierta hora. SUSTANTIVO

week/semana Unidad de tiempo que corresponde a siete días. SUSTANTIVO

work/trabajo Una forma de lograr que se hagan las cosas. SUSTANTIVO

year/año Medida de tiempo que corresponde a 12 meses. SUSTANTIVO

Index

This index lists the pages on which topics appear in this book. Page numbers followed by *m* refer to maps. Page numbers followed by *p* refer to photographs. Page numbers followed by *c* refer to charts or graphs. Page numbers followed by *t* refer to timelines. Bold page numbers indicate vocabulary definitions. The terms *See* and *See also* direct the reader to alternate entries.

Credits

Text Acknowledgments

CBS Interactive Inc.

Quote by Ruby Bridges from "40 Years After, Ruby Bridges Fights On" from CBS News, November 14, 2000. Copyright © CBS Interactive, Inc.

Images

Cover

Sappington Todd/Getty Images;

Front Matter

Copyright Page: Rachid Dahnoun/Aurora Open RF/Alamy Stock Photo; iii: Dr. Albert M. Camarillo; iii: Dr. James B. Kracht; iii: Dr. Kathy Swan; iii: Dr. Linda B. Bennett; iii: Elfrieda H. Hiebert; iii: Jim Cummins; iii: Kathy Tuchman Glass; iii: Paul Apodaca; iii: Dr. Shirley A. James Hanshaw; iii: Warren J. Blumenfeld; iii: Xiaojian Zhao; Xii: Bettmann/Getty Images; XiiiB: National Baseball Hall of Fame Library/Major League Baseball Platinum/Getty Images; XiiiT: NASA Photo/Alamy Stock Photo; xvi: Dorothea Lange/Library of Congress Prints and Photographs Division[LC-USF33-015330-M2]; xviiiL: Tomas Abad/Alamy Stock Photo; xviiiR: B. Christopher/Alamy Stock Photo; xix: US National Archives/Alamy Stock Photo; SSH01: Kenkistler/Shutterstock; SSH02: Comstock/Exactostock-1557/Superstock; SSH03L: Nicolette Wollentin/123RF; SSH03R: Juniors Bildarchiv GmbH/Alamy Stock Photo; SSH04T: Wavebreakmedia/Shutterstock; SSH04L: Neale Clark/Robertharding/Alamy Stock Photo; SSH04R: Kevin Schafer/Alamy Stock Photo; SSH05L: Natalia Bratslavsky/Shutterstock; SSH05R: Robert Landau/Corbis Documentary/Getty Images; SSH05T: EverythingLincoln.com; SSH05B: Pearson Education, Inc.; SSH06: Bettmann/Getty Images; SSH07: Pearson Education, Inc.;

Chapter 01

001: Juice Images Ltd/Getty Images 005: Fstop123/E+/Getty Images; 006: Kablonk/Golden Pixels LLC/Alamy Stock Photo; 008: Unguryanu/Shutterstock; 009: Micromonkey/Fotolia; 010: US National Archives/Alamy Stock Photo; 014B: Bettmann/Getty Images; 014T: Andrey_Kuzmin/Shutterstock; 015: Srijaroen/Shutterstock; 017: Steve Skjold/Alamy Stock Photo; 019: Arthur Schatz/The Life Picture Collection/Getty Images; 020: Zuma Press, Inc./Alamy Stock Photo; 021: John Van Hasselt/Sygma/Getty Images; 026: Tomas Abad/Alamy Stock Photo; 027: B. Christopher/Alamy Stock Photo; 028B: Nick Ut/AP Images; 028T: Keith Birmingham/Zuma Press/Newscom; 030: KidStock/Blend Images/Getty Images;

Chapter 02

032-033: Ethel Wolvovitz/Alamy Stock Photo; 039B: Matej Hudovernik/Shutterstock; 039T: John Hyde/Perspectives/Getty Images; 040: Charlie Neuman/U-T San Diego/ZUMA Press Inc/Alamy Stock Photo; 041: MaxyM/Shutterstock; 042: Niday Picture Library/Alamy Stock Photo; 043: Brian Erickson/Fotolia; 044: Matt Tilghman/Shutterstock; 045: Ian Dagnall Commercial Collection/Alamy Stock Photo; 046B: Yurchello108/Fotolia; 046T: Ra3rn/Shutterstock; 047B: Three Lions/Hulton Royals Collection/Getty Images; 047T: Yurchello108/Fotolia; 049: Dann Tardif/Corbis/Getty Images; 050: Ted Foxx/Alamy Stock Photo; 051: Ariel Skelley/Blend Images/Getty Images; 052L: Syntheticmessiah/Fotolia; 052R: Hurst Photo/Shutterstock; 053B: Monkey Business Images/Shutterstock; 053T: GL Archive/Alamy Stock Photo; 054B: Trekandphoto/Fotolia; 054T: B. Christopher/Alamy Stock Photo; 055BR: 123RF; 055C: John Hyde/Perspectives/Getty Images; 055TL: Shnycel/Shutterstock; 55B: Matej Hudovernik/Shutterstock;

Chapter 03

058: Yvette Cardozo/Photolibrary/Getty Images; 063BL: Roman Sigaev/Shutterstock; 063BR: Galushko Sergey/Shutterstock; 063C: 123RF; 063T: Eurobanks/iStock/Getty Images; 064BL: Bakhtiarzein/Fotolia; 064R: Harrychoi/TongRo Images/Alamy Stock Photo; 064TC: Tpfeller/Shutterstock; 065B: Buddy Mays/Alamy Stock Photo; 065T: H. Armstrong Roberts/ClassicStock/Alamy Stock Photo; 067: Myrleen Pearson/Alamy Stock Photo; 070: H. Armstrong Roberts/ClassicStock/Alamy Stock Photo; 071: Stefano Politi Markovina/Alamy Stock Photo; 072: Stockbroker/MBI/Alamy Stock Photo; 073BL: H. ARMSTRONG ROBERTS/ClassicStock/Alamy Stock Photo; 073BR: Erik Isakson/Tetra Images/Alamy Stock Photo; 073T: Nejron Photo/Shutterstock; 074: SuperStock; 075: Semen Lihodeev/Alamy Stock Photo; 076B: Jeff Greenberg/UIG/Getty Images; 076T: Photo Researchers, Inc/Alamy Stock Photo; 078BL: North Wind Picture Archives/Alamy Stock Photo; 078BR: Hongqi Zhang/Alamy Stock Photo; 078T: Karen Struthers/Alamy Stock Photo; 078TB: Mark Andersen/RubberBall/Alamy Stock Photo; 078TC: Wavebreakmedia/Shutterstock;

Chapter 04

080: Eric Raptosh/Hill Street Studios/Blend Images/Getty Images; 086: Robert Landau/Alamy Stock Photo; 088: KidStock/Blend Images/Age Fotostock; 090: Jamie Pham Photography/Alamy Stock Photo; 097: Stockbroker/MBI/Alamy Stock Photo; 098: John Crowe/Alamy Stock Photo; 099: Tom Wang/Shutterstock; 101BC: Haryadi CH/Shutterstock; 101BL: Jim Mills/Fotolia; 101BR: Rnl/Shutterstock; 101T: Mark J Hunt/Getty Images; 103L: Dorothea Lange/Library of Congress Prints and Photographs Division[LC-USF34-021774-C]; 103R: Education Images/UIG/Getty Images; 104L: Image

I go am to the
store

I am go to the store

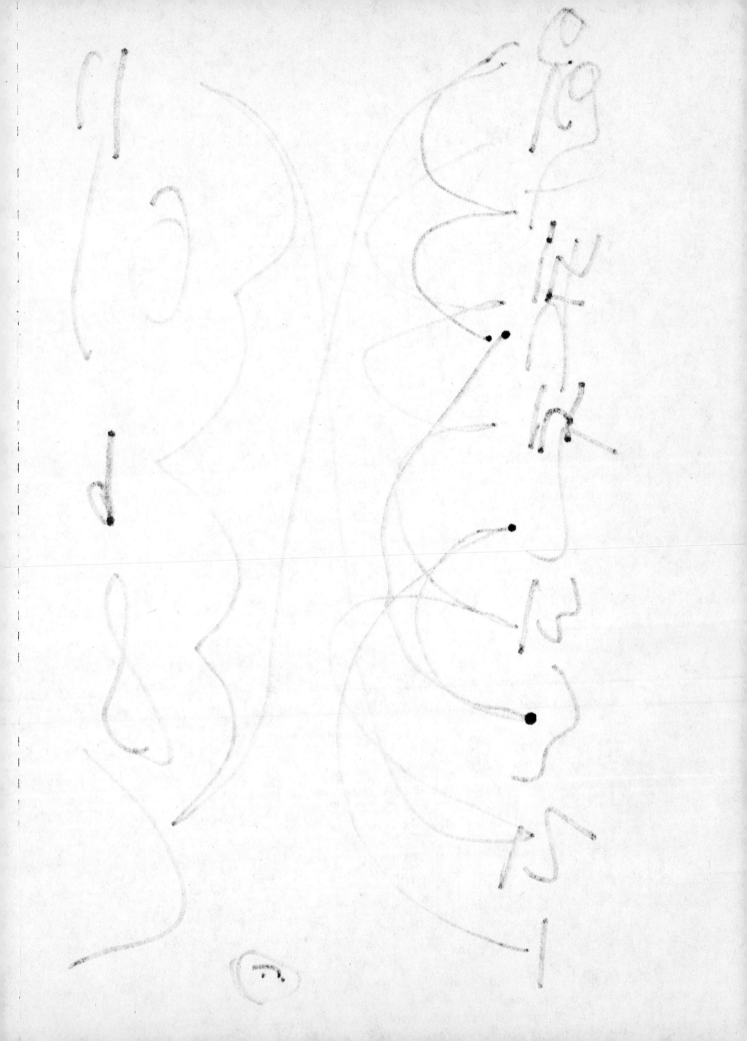

look how to get on.

Now got on the but the but ♡

♡ Dan got on the bus the bus
took him to school.

2 + 5 = 7

2 + 5 = 3

20 + 5 = 25

200 + 5 = 25

200 + 5 = 35

50 + 30 = 20

20 + 20 = 40

500

1 + 1 = 1

5

1 + 1 = 11

100 + 10

50 + 10 = 11

100

$5+2=7$

$1+2=3$ $60+1=61$

$20+30=50$ $200+2=32$

$11+1=4$ $200+3$ $70+1=205$

$11+30=100+6$ 106

$35+1$ $9+00$

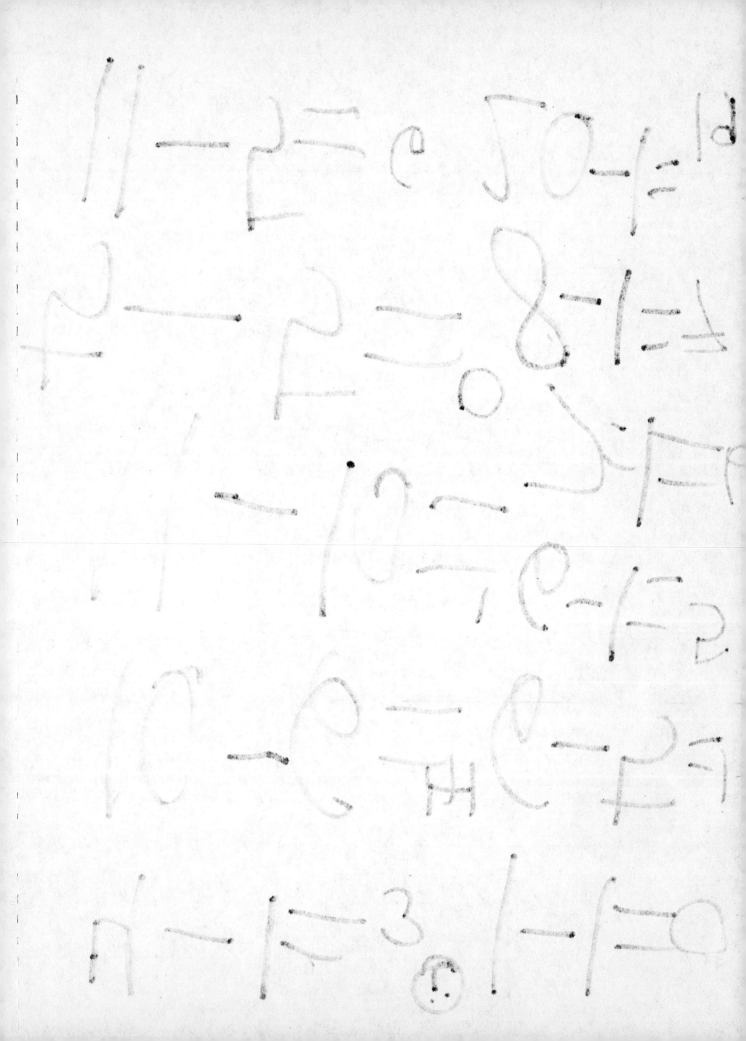

20 − 1 = 19

11 − 5 = 6   9 − 2 = 7

8 − 1 = 7

11 − 1 = 10   6 − 1 = 5

10 − 9 = ？   6 − ？ = ？   15 − 4 = ？

4 − 1 = 3   1 − 1 = 0